trade mantra

MASTER 80+ STRATEGIES USED BY THE TOP 1% OF THE TRADERS GLOBALLY

ATULESH KUMAR SINHA

INDIA · SINGAPORE · MALAYSIA

ISBN

Hardcase 979-8-89724-916-9
Paperback 979-8-89673-489-5

Dedication

A RIGHT PATH WILL TURN A GOOD GAIN.

This book stands as a symbol of gratitude, love, and hope - a tribute to the people who have shaped my life and the traders who inspire me every day. "Trade Mantra" is a labor of love, a culmination of countless hours of study, experimentation, and passion for the art and science of trading. It would not have been possible without the unwavering support, inspiration, and belief of the people who mean the world to me.

My sincere apology to my loved ones who got limited time during this process and let me remind you my whole world is not complete without my beautiful wife, lovely child, sweet friends and loveable parents. They are my actual motivation behind the book and always a hero in my life.

To my mentor **Mr. Vivekananda Sinha**, who has always created a roadmap with the right guidance in the skills, encouraged to communicate through this book, inspiration to get the courage about the risks in life as a positive note. Your support will always hold a strong guide throughout my life.

We are always thankful to the publisher, editor, well wishers, readers who have given the platform to build a base of this book. True insight of the traders will always be efficient when used in right measurement which has been mentioned in the book.

Table of Contents

Warning

Did you dream Big Today???
A TRADER WHO SITS IDEAL ARE NOT WELCOME HERE.

Yes, you read it correctly. There is no longer room for the inactive trader to trade.

Are you a student, homemaker, professional, coach, or proprietor? We don't care about the background, as our aim is to make you fall for the right path. It is a token of love and to fulfill your dreams with handy tricks in trading. Here we will learn more about "Trade Mantra". This is not a generic guide full of outdated, surface-level tips. Instead, it's a powerhouse of 89 meticulously crafted trading strategies designed to arm you with the tools and knowledge to dominate the markets.

Each chapter unlocks a new layer of technical analysis mastery—moving averages, MACD, RSI, Bollinger Bands, Ichimoku Clouds, and more—all tailored for traders hungry for precision, control, and profitability. These are not cookie-cutter methods but battle-tested techniques that adapt to dynamic market conditions. Awaiting for the right content, block your seats to grasp more about "Power of momentum indicators, Discover secret confluence zone, Master the art of trend-following, breakout hunting, and reversal spotting, Combine advanced tools like Renko charts, fractals, and smoothing technique".

What will be the output?? - You will be gaining a perfect direction as a trained trader by finishing this book, but for this we have one condition: "Purchase it." This book will be your guide, and we assure you will connect with us again with the feedback and more insights. If you lose the opportunity, then you may stake your own growth as a trader.

This book demands to use your time as investment; no shortcuts, strategies, views about finance markets, skills with a roadmap, and much more will be covered here and profitable to avoid the risks that are already mentioned as a warning. Your sincere approach will change your life, but your overconfidence to alter the strategy will bear a loss. Remember to follow the steps as mentioned clearly in the concepts and do not manipulate it with own strategy - "Money needs tricks, not a market-wise move." Prove me wrong, if you can by attempting it and challenge with your own ideas.

Take the plunge, and you might unlock insights that could redefine your financial journey.

Time has begun with the metamorphosis, and your journey to commercial power begins now. Try it, and you won't be able to go back to your normal ideas. Trapped as a trader...

GET STARTED WITH THIS STRATEGY AND CHECK THE PROFIT MARGIN.

Acknowledgement

The best part of the book is this page wherein we get the chance to thank all our supporters, readers, and the team behind our success. My heart is overwhelmed with the personal and professional strategies that were covered in the "Trade Mantra" book. The expertise, knowledge, testaments of sleepless nights, unending thoughts, and brief explanation has been covered in this book with the help of traders and contributors who guided the strategies which are inherited here.

My heartfelt gratitude towards my wife, **Neha**. Two year old daughter, **Riddhi** and my late **father** and **mother** who are great contributors in my life from molding me into a visionary. Their deep thoughts behind using the great experience in the disciplined way, thirst for knowledge, and resilience was a result of this book. My journey crossed paths to success when they are part of my life and today I am proud of this achievement. A special token of thanks to my mentor - **Vivekananda Sinha** Sir who has made me realize the worth of knowledge required to empower traders which influenced my journey.

To all the **Traders** out there - this book is for you. Your relentless pursuit of knowledge and your determination to succeed in the ever - challenging world of trading inspire me every day. I hope the strategies in these pages provide you with the tools and confidence to navigate the markets with greater precision and clarity. To all the authors, educators, and trading professionals whose insights and teachings have shaped my understanding of technical analysis a big thank to you. This book builds on the foundation of knowledge laid by those who have come before me, and I am grateful for their contributions to the field.

Lastly, a thankful note to **Notion Press** for providing me necessary resources and support to release this book, thank you for your dedication, expertise, and hard work in bringing this project to fruition. Your efforts have helped transform my ideas into a resource that I hope will benefit traders for years to come. This book is the culmination of collective wisdom, personal experiences, and unmalleable support from all corners of my life. To everyone who has been a part of this journey, I extend my deepest gratitude.

I hereby acknowledge this book is not to buy and sell stocks but a guidance to trust yourself and be confident using these strategies and generate profit with your own risk of knowledge. Our mission is to become a supporter to the trader and give a helping hand as an asset.

Preface

Trading and understanding is not everyone's cup of tea, it is said by local people as they want to trade safely through the advisors. Our journey was alike and we have also got healed with the strategies which were wretched by the losses.

Trade Mantra will be a toolkit with all the experiences which are already faced in the journey to learn trade and successfully grow ahead in the career. Our aim is to be guidance and knowledge only, not to compete with anyone for the following patterns. A trader needs to be inspired by self risk of taking ownership for profits and losses with the market strategy. As a trader, we have experienced firsthand the thrill of a perfectly timed trade and the frustration of unexpected losses. Through it all, one thing has become abundantly clear: success in trading is not about luck; it's about strategy, discipline, and the willingness to learn continuously.

Trade Mantra, is the result of years of exploration, study, and experimentation in the world of trading. It represents a consolidation of everything that has been learned about market behavior, technical indicators, and the art of decision - making under uncertainty. Our goal is to provide traders - beginners and seasoned professionals alike - with a powerful arsenal of strategies to navigate the complexities of the stock market.

The strategies in Trade Mantra are not generic. They are the product of rigorous testing and refinement, designed to address specific market conditions and trading styles. From moving averages to Bollinger Bands, from MACD to Ichimoku Clouds, each chapter delves into unique techniques that can enhance your ability to spot trends, identify reversals, and manage risk effectively.

To reading, learning and motivating in the journey of trading there were many ups and downs which resulted in this book. Our sincere and grateful thanks would be for the persons who always shouldered me in dark times and raised me as a star to navigate readers through this book. My gratitude and bow to people like family (Loveable wife Neha and sweet daughter Riddhi), friends and mentor - Vivekananda Sinha. Their approach was always remarkable which paved an inspirational thought towards recreating the experiences in joy. So, this book is like a soul clubbed with professional and personal attachment which will be helpful to everyone.

To all the traders reading this: I understand your struggles and aspirations. The markets can be unforgiving, but it also reward perseverance and preparation. This book is my way of sharing the knowledge that has helped me navigate this journey and, I hope, will help you too.

As you turn these pages, approach them with an open mind and a willingness to experiment. The path to trading success is not a straight line - it's a journey of continuous learning and growth. Let this book be your companion in that journey.

For more information, please visit **trademantra.atuleshsinha.com**

Yes, Any body can trade with **Trade Mantra!**

Happy trading, and may your strategies bring you wealth & success.

Introduction

Trading in today's world has never been more accessible. Thanks to advances in technology, the rise of user - friendly trading platforms, and a wealth of online resources, virtually anyone can participate in financial markets. Gone are the days when trading was reserved for professionals on Wall Street or large institutional investors. Today, anyone with an internet connection, a Smartphone, and basic financial literacy can enter the markets and work towards building a supplementary or even primary income stream.

For the lower - or middle - class employee, the stock market offers a realistic opportunity to break free from financial limitations. With proper education, disciplined strategies, and a small initial investment, trading can serve as a path toward financial growth, helping individuals supplement their monthly income, save for future goals, or even achieve long - term wealth. The barriers to entry have significantly reduced, making trading a viable option for people from all walks of life.

Swing trading, a powerful and dynamic trading approach, is the art of capturing short -to medium - term price movements in financial markets. Whether you're trading stocks, forex, commodities, or crypto currencies, swing trading offers the potential for consistent profits without the constant screen - watching associated with day trading. By focusing on capturing "swings" in price action, this method blends technical analysis, risk management, and strategy design into a cohesive system tailored to modern markets.

This book is designed as a comprehensive guide to mastering swing trading. With 15 meticulously curated chapters, it introduces you to 89 actionable strategies, ranging from classic techniques to innovative methods adapted for today's fast - evolving trading environment. Each strategy is crafted with practical insights, making it accessible for traders of all skill levels - whether you're a beginner seeking structure or an experienced trader refining your edge.

Why Swing Trading?

Swing trading strikes a balance between the fast pace of day trading and the patience required for long - term investing. It allows traders to take advantage of significant market moves over a few days to weeks, leveraging technical indicators, patterns, and momentum shifts. The flexibility of this style means you don't need to be glued to your screens all day, making it ideal for those balancing trading with other commitments.

The strategies in this book cater to diverse trading styles, market conditions, and risk appetites. From trend - following techniques to contrarian approaches, each strategy is detailed with entry and exit rules, risk management guidelines, and tips for adapting to different market environments.

What's Inside?

The book is organized into 15 chapters, each focusing on a specific category of technical indicators or trading systems:

- **Moving Average Marvels:** Master the fundamentals with six powerful moving average strategies, from simple crossovers to advanced fractal adaptive systems. These strategies provide a solid foundation for identifying trends and optimizing entries.
- **MACD Mastery:** Explore the versatility of the MACD indicator with eight strategies that cover trend - following, divergence analysis, and multi - indicator confluence. This chapter is a goldmine for traders seeking precision in timing.

- **RSI Riches:** Learn to harness the RSI's power in five strategies that highlight overbought/oversold conditions, divergences, and trendline breakouts. Special focus is given to combining RSI with Heikin - Ashi smoothing and volume confirmation.
- **Stochastics Setups:** Dive into the stochastic oscillator with five setups that focus on momentum, divergence, and multi - indicator smoothing.
- **Ichimoku Clouds:** Gain an edge with six strategies built around this holistic indicator, perfect for identifying trends, reversals, and dynamic support and resistance.
- **And More:** Each subsequent chapter builds on these foundations, introducing innovative ways to trade with indicators like Bollinger Bands, Awesome Oscillators, ADX, Aroon, OBV, and CMO, as well as alternative methods like Fibonacci retracements, ATR breakouts, and VWAP - based systems.

A Unique Approach

What sets this book apart is its structured yet adaptable approach. Each chapter not only explains the strategies but also emphasizes their practical application in real - world markets. You'll learn how to combine indicators, adapt to different timeframes, and refine your methods for various asset classes. Moreover, the inclusion of Renko charts, Heikin - Ashi candlesticks, and other advanced techniques ensures a fresh perspective on swing trading.

The Path to Mastery

Swing trading is more than just a set of strategies - it's a mindset. This book equips you with the tools, knowledge, and confidence to navigate the markets with discipline and consistency. Whether your goal is to achieve financial independence, diversify your income streams, or simply improve your trading acumen, this guide is your companion on the path to mastery.

Most interesting thing about this book is, that you don't have to read in serial, you can read any strategy in any sequence as per your will.

Consistency and discipline is more important than sequence to get more from this book.

Get ready to dive deep, experiment, and develop a personalized approach that aligns with your trading goals. Let's embark on this exciting journey into the world of swing trading!

Moving Average Marvels

Moving averages are the backbone of technical analysis, providing a clear picture of price trends and smoothing out market noise. This chapter introduces you to six beginner-friendly strategies that leverage the power of moving averages. You'll start with the Simple MA Cross Strategy, which identifies trend reversals when two moving averages cross. The Exponential MA Pullback Strategy helps you spot pullbacks within a trend for high-probability entries. Triple MA Confluence Filter adds another layer of confirmation, combining three moving averages to validate trend strength. The MA Envelope Breakouts strategy focuses on price breaking above or below dynamic bands to signal momentum. With Variable MA Crossovers, you'll learn to adapt to different market conditions. Finally, the Fractal Adaptive MA Signals use fractals to fine-tune entry points. By mastering these strategies, you can stay on the right side of the market and avoid common pitfalls.

1

Simple MA Cross Strategy

A Simple moving average crossover is a popular trading strategy that uses two or more simple moving averages to find buy and sell signals. The basic idea behind this strategy is to use two simple moving averages of different lengths and look for a crossover between them. When the shorter - term moving average exceeds the longer - term moving average, it is considered a bullish signal. For example, for positional trading, you can use a 21 - period simple moving average for the short term and a 50 - period simple moving average for the long term.

Entry:

Bullish Signal: Enter a long position when the short - term simple moving average (21 periods MA) crosses above the long - term simple moving average (50 periods MA), indicating a bullish crossover.

Bearish Signal: Enter a short position when the short - term simple moving average (21 periods MA) crosses below the long - term simple moving average (50 periods MA), signaling a bearish crossover.

You can confirm crossover signals with other indicators, such as RSI, MACD, etc., or use price action analysis (Breakout) for more confirmations.

Stop Loss:

The stop loss should be based on the previous Swing Low/Swing High, ATR (Average True Range), MACD, or any other indicator.

Exit Rules:

Profit Target: Your profit target should be based on your risk - reward ratio. It could be a specific percentage gain or a resistance/support level.

Trailing Stop: You can trail stop - loss to maximize your profit and ride the total momentum as the price moves in your favor.

Risk Management:

Position Sizing: Determine the appropriate size based on your risk tolerance and account size. You should park only 5% of your Capital at a time.

Risk - Reward Ratio: Ensure that your potential profit is significantly greater than your potential loss for each trade. Keep your Risk - Reward ratio at least 1:2.

Example:

For a Bullish crossover example, refer to the attached chart of BAYER Crop Science. 20 SMA (green line) crossed above 50 SMA (Orange line) on May 11, 2023. We take entry (buy stock) at 4250.00 with a stop loss at 3900.00 (Previous Swing low/Support) and a Target of 5000.00 (Near Previous Swing high/Resistance). The Risk: reward is almost 1:2, and the target hits on Sep 05, 2023, with 17.65% profit from the deployed Capital.

2

Exponential Moving Average (EMA) Pullback Strategy

The Exponential Moving Average (EMA) is similar to simple moving averages but gives more weight to recent prices. It reacts quicker to price changes compared to the simple moving averages.

Entry:

Bullish Signal: Enter a long position when the stock is in an uptrend, and after going far from EMA, the Price comes (pull back) to the EMA.

Bearish Signal: Enter a short position when the stock is in a downtrend, and after going far from the EMA, the Price returns to the EMA (Pullback).

You can confirm crossover signals with other indicators, such as RSI, MACD, etc., or use price action analysis (Breakout) for more confirmations.

Stop Loss:

The stop loss should be based on the previous Swing Low/Swing High, ATR (Average True Range), MACD, or any other indicator.

Exit Rules:

Profit Target: Your profit target should be based on your risk - reward ratio. It could be a specific percentage gain or a resistance/support level.

Trailing Stop: You can trail stop - loss to maximize your profit and ride the total momentum as the price moves in your favor.

Risk Management:

Position Sizing: Determine the appropriate size based on your risk tolerance and account size. You should park only 5% of your Capital at a time.

Risk - Reward Ratio: Ensure that your potential profit is significantly greater than your potential loss for each trade. Keep your Risk - Reward ratio at least 1:2.

Example:

For a Bullish crossover example, refer to the attached chart of ABB India. The stock is in an uptrend. The Price went far from the 21 EMA, then Pulled Back and closed below the 21 EMA. On 06th May - 24, the Price closed above the previous swing high. We took entry (buy stock) at 6940.00 with a stop loss at 6240.00 (Previous Swing low/Support) and a Target of 8350.00 (1:2 R: R). The Risk: reward ratio is almost 1:2, and the Target hit on 16th May - 24 with a 20.32% profit on deployed Capital.

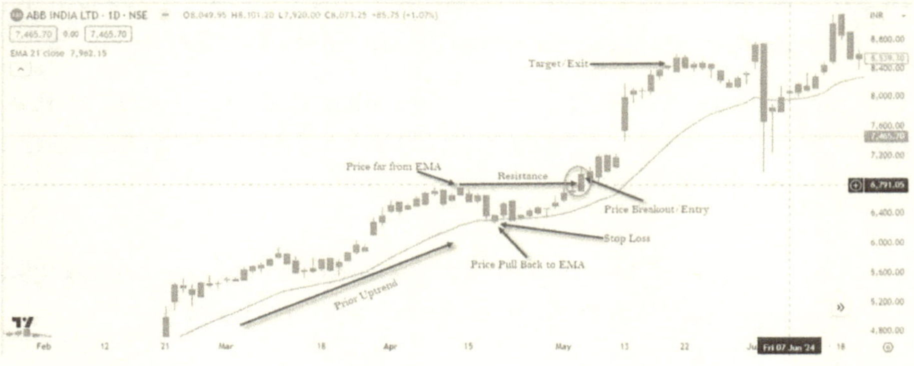

3

Triple MA Confluence Filter

The Moving Average Convergence strategy is based on the idea that various moving averages have different sensitivity levels to price movements. Shorter - term moving averages react more quickly to changes in Price, while longer - term moving averages respond more slowly. When combined, they offer a more comprehensive view of the overall trend.

Entry:

Bullish Signal: Enter a long position when a shorter - term moving average crosses above a longer - term moving average.

Bearish Signal: Enter a short position when a shorter - term moving average crosses below a longer - term moving average.

You can confirm crossover signals with other indicators, such as RSI, MACD, etc., or use price action analysis (Breakout) for more confirmations.

Stop Loss:

Stop loss should be based on the previous Swing Low/Swing High, ATR (Average True Range), MACD, or any other indicator.

Exit Rules:

Profit Target: Your profit target should be based on your risk - reward ratio. It could be a specific percentage gain or a resistance or support level.

Trailing Stop: You can trail stop - loss to maximize your profit and ride the total momentum as the price moves in your favor.

Risk Management:

Position Sizing: Determine the appropriate size based on your risk tolerance and account size. You should park only 5% of your Capital at a time.

Risk - Reward Ratio: Ensure that your potential profit is significantly greater than your potential loss for each trade. Keep your Risk - Reward ratio at least 1:2.

Example:

For the Bullish MA confluence example, refer to the attached chart of Aditya Birla Capital. The 20 MA of stock was trading below 50 & 100 MA for some time; on 06th Feb - 2024, 20 MA crossed above 50 & 100 MA. On 07th Feb - 24, the Price closes above the previous swing high. We take entry (buy stock) at 187.00 with a stop loss at 160.00 (Previous Swing low/ Support) and a Target of 241.00 (1:2 R: R). The Risk: Reward is almost 1:2, and Target hit on 29th Apr - 24 with 28.88% profit on deployed Capital.

4

MA Envelope Breakouts

Moving Average Envelopes are percentage - based envelopes set above and below a moving average. The moving average (20 SMA in our example), which forms the base for this indicator, can be a simple or exponential moving average. Each envelope is set to the same percentage (10% in our example) above or below the moving average. This range creates parallel bands that follow price action. With a moving average as the base, Moving Average Envelopes can be used as a trend - following indicator. Beyond simply trend following, we use the envelopes to identify overbought and oversold levels when the trend is relatively flat.

Entry:

Bullish Signal: Enter a long position when a stock breaks out above a lower band, indicating bullish strength after a bearish movement.

Bearish Signal: Enter a short position when a stock breaks down the upper band, indicating reduced strength after a bullish trend.

You can confirm crossover signals with other indicators, such as RSI, MACD, etc., or use price action analysis (Breakout) for more confirmations.

Stop Loss:

The stop loss should be based on the previous Swing Low/Swing High, ATR (Average True Range), MACD, or any other indicator.

Exit Rules:

Profit Target: Your profit target should be based on your risk - reward ratio. It could be a specific percentage gain or a resistance/support level.

Trailing Stop: You can trail stop - loss to maximize your profit and ride the total momentum as the price moves in your favor.

Risk Management:

Position Sizing: Determine the appropriate size based on your risk tolerance and account size. You should park only 5% of your Capital at a time.

Risk - Reward Ratio: Ensure that your potential profit is significantly greater than your potential loss for each trade. Keep your Risk - Reward ratio at least 1:2.

Example:

For Bullish MA Envelope Breakouts, refer to the attached chart of ABFRL. The stock closes below the lower band on 13th Mar - 2024 and reverses afterward; on 01st Apr - 2024, stock closes above the Upper Band, and on 02nd Apr - 2024, the Price breaks out of the previous swing high. We take entry (buy stock) at 236.00 with a stop loss at 198.00 (Previous Swing low/ Support) and a Target of 312.00 (1:2 R: R). The Risk: Reward is almost 1:2, and Target hit on 06th Jun - 24 with 32.20% profit on deployed Capital.

5

Variable MA Crossovers

A variable moving average (VMA) is an exponential moving average (EMA) that can automatically regulate its smoothing percentage based on market volatility. The idea behind the VMA crossover is to dynamically adapt moving averages to a trend's volatility. Its sensitivity improves by assigning more weight to the ongoing data, generating a better signal for short and long - term markets.

Entry:

Bullish Signal: Enter a long position when a short - term (9 EMA in our case) VMA crosses above a long - term (21 EMA in our case) VMA.

Bearish Signal: Enter a short position when a short - term (9 EMA in our case) VMA crosses below a long - term (21 EMA in our case) VMA.

You can confirm crossover signals with other indicators, such as RSI, MACD, etc., or use price action analysis (Breakout) for more confirmations.

Stop Loss:

The stop loss should be based on the previous Swing Low/Swing High, ATR (Average True Range), MACD, or any other indicator.

Exit Rules:

Profit Target: Your profit target should be based on your risk - reward ratio. It could be a specific percentage gain or a resistance/support level.

Trailing Stop: You can trail stop - loss to maximize your profit and ride the total momentum as the price moves in your favor.

Risk Management:

Position Sizing: Determine the appropriate size based on your risk tolerance and account size. You should park only 5% of your Capital at a time.

Risk - Reward Ratio: Ensure that your potential profit is significantly greater than your potential loss for each trade. Keep your Risk - Reward ratio at least 1:2.

Example:

For Bullish VMA Crossover, refer to the attached chart of ACC. The 9 VMA (Green Line) crosses above 21 VMA (Red Line) on Dec 18, 2023, and we are waiting for price action. On 02nd Jan - 2024, the stock broke out of the previous swing high. We take entry (buy stock) at 2255.00 with a stop loss at 2040.00 (Previous Swing low/Support) and a Target of 2690.00 (1:2 R: R). The Risk: Reward is almost 1:2, and Target hit on 16th Feb - 24 with 19.29% profit on deployed Capital.

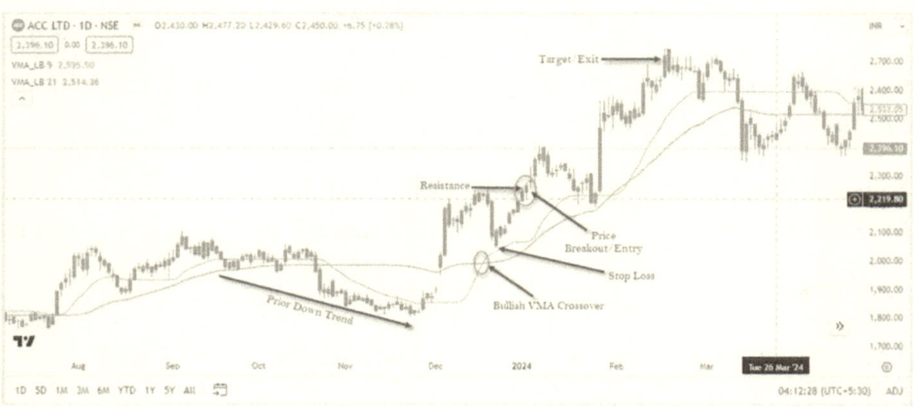

6

Fractal Adaptive MA Signals

The FRAMA strategy is a technical analysis tool developed by John Ehlers. We use this indicator to identify trending markets and measure the trend's strength. FRAMA is a moving average that adjusts itself in response to the market's volatility. This adjustment makes it more adaptive to changing market conditions than traditional moving averages. The FRAMA strategy works by measuring the rate of change in the security price over time. When the rate of change is high, the stock is in an uptrend. When the rate of change is low, the stock is in a downtrend. The FRAMA indicator uses an adaptive moving average to determine when these trends occur. The FRAMA strategy's main benefits are its ability to identify trends more accurately than traditional moving averages, its adaptability to changing market conditions, and its ability to measure the strength of a trend. We can use FRAMA to confirm price movements and provide entry and exit points for trades.

Entry:

Bullish Signal: Enter a long position when the stock price exceeds the FRAMA line.

Bearish Signal: Enter a short position when the stock price exceeds the FRAMA line.

You can confirm crossover signals with other indicators, such as RSI, MACD, etc., or use price action analysis (Breakout) for more confirmations.

Stop Loss:

The stop loss should be based on the previous Swing Low/Swing High, ATR (Average True Range), MACD, or any other indicator.

Exit Rules:

Profit Target: Your profit target should be based on your risk - reward ratio. It could be a specific percentage gain or a resistance/support level.

Trailing Stop: You can trail stop - loss to maximize your profit and ride the total momentum as the price moves in your favor.

Risk Management:

Position Sizing: Determine the appropriate size based on your risk tolerance and account size. You should park only 5% of your Capital at a time.

Risk - Reward Ratio: Ensure that your potential profit is significantly greater than your potential loss for each trade. Keep your Risk - Reward ratio at least 1:2.

Example:

For Bullish FRAMA, refer to the attached chart of ACI. On 30th Jan - 2024, the script price crossed above the FRAMA line and broke out of the previous swing high. We take entry (buy stock) at 630.00 with a stop loss at 590.00 (Previous Swing low/Support) and a Target of 710.00 (1:2 R: R). The Risk: Reward is almost 1:2, and Target hit on 19th Feb - 24 with 12.70% profit on deployed Capital.

MACD Mastery

The MACD (Moving Average Convergence Divergence) indicator is a versatile tool for tracking momentum and trend strength. In this chapter, you'll explore eight powerful MACD strategies. The MACD Trend-Following strategy helps you ride strong trends, while the MACD Centerline Crossover identifies shifts in momentum as the MACD crosses zero. The MACD Divergence System teaches you to spot early reversal signals by comparing price action and MACD behavior. Use the MACD Histogram Strategy to identify subtle shifts in momentum before they're reflected in price. For greater accuracy, the Combined MACD/RSI Signals strategy merges MACD and RSI to confirm entries and exits. The Triple EMA/MACD Confluence strategy integrates moving averages for multi-layered validation. Learn to trade unique setups with the MACD Renko Entry and the powerful MACD/Stochastics/RSI Combo for comprehensive analysis. These strategies will help you capitalize on momentum shifts, confirm trends, and spot potential reversals with confidence.

7

MACD (Moving Average Convergence Divergence) Trend - Following Strategy

Moving Average Convergence Divergence or MACD is a momentum indicator that shows the relationship between 2 EMAs, i.e., 12 & 26 EMA of the underline. Convergence happens when two EMAs move toward one another, while Divergence occurs when two EMAs move away.

Entry:

Bullish Signal: Enter a long position when the MACD line crosses above the signal line, generating a bullish crossover signal.

Bearish Signal: Enter a short position when the MACD line crosses below the signal line, producing a bearish crossover signal.

Use the MACD histogram to visualize momentum strength and Divergence between the MACD and signal lines for additional confirmation.

Stop Loss:

The stop loss should be based on the previous Swing Low/Swing High, ATR (Average True Range), or any other indicator.

Exit Rules:

Profit Target: The profit target is based on your risk - reward ratio. It could be a specific percentage gain or a resistance or support level.

Trailing Stop: You can trail stop - loss to maximize your profit and ride the total momentum as the price moves in your favor.

Risk Management:

Position Sizing: Determine the appropriate size based on your risk tolerance and account size. You should park only 5% of your Capital at a time.

Risk - Reward Ratio: Ensure that your potential profit is significantly greater than your potential loss for each trade. Keep your Risk - Reward ratio at least 1:2.

Example:

For a Bullish example, refer to the attached chart of ABB. The MACD line (Blue) crosses the Signal line (Orange) on Feb 21, 24. Also, the Price broke out of the previous swing. We took an entry (buy stock) at 5000.00 with a stop loss at 4300.00 (Previous Swing low/Support) and a Target of 6500.00. The Risk: reward ratio is almost 1:2, and the Target was hit on Apr 01, 24, with a 30% profit on deployed Capital.

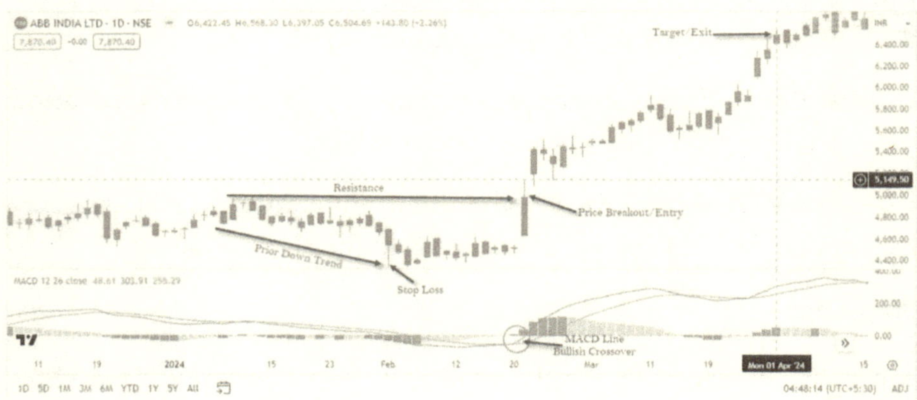

8

MACD Centerline Crossover

MACD is a momentum indicator that shows the relationship between two EMAs, i.e., the 12 and 26 EMA of the underline. Convergence happens when two EMAs move toward one another, while Divergence occurs when two EMAs move away from each other. The MACD line crossing above zero (Centre line) is bullish.

Entry:

Bullish Signal: Enter a long position when the MACD line crosses above the Centre line (zero), generating a bullish crossover signal.

Bearish Signal: Enter a short position when the MACD line crosses below the Centre line (zero), producing a bearish crossover signal.

Use the MACD histogram to visualize momentum strength and Divergence between the MACD and signal lines for additional confirmation.

Stop Loss:

The stop loss should be based on the previous Swing Low/Swing High, ATR (Average True Range), or any other indicator.

Exit Rules:

Profit Target: Your profit target should be based on your risk - reward ratio. It could be a specific percentage gain or a resistance/support level.

Trailing Stop: You can trail stop - loss to maximize your profit and ride the total momentum as the price moves in your favor.

Risk Management:

Position Sizing: Determine the appropriate size based on your risk tolerance and account size. You should park only 5% of your Capital at a time.

Risk - Reward Ratio: Ensure that your potential profit is significantly greater than your potential loss for each trade. Keep your Risk - Reward ratio at least 1:2.

Example:

For a Bullish example, refer to the attached chart of APL Apollo Tubes. The MACD line (Blue) crosses the Centre line (zero) on 09th Jun - 2023, and the price breakout of the previous swing is on 12th Jun - 2023. We take entry (buy stock) at 1265.00 with a stop loss at 1045.00 (Previous Swing low/Support) and a Target of 1710.00. The Risk: The reward is almost 1:2, and the target was hit on Sep 01, 2023, with 35.18% profit on the deployed Capital.

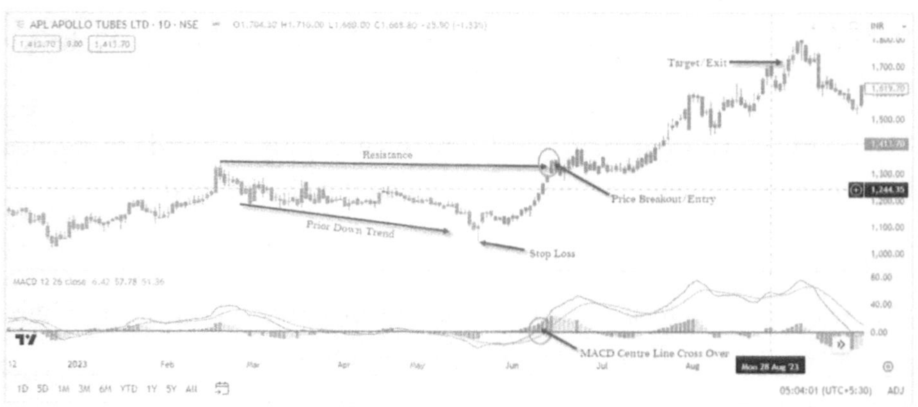

9

MACD Divergence Strategy

The MACD Divergence occurs when the Price creates higher highs and the MACD creates lower lows, indicating a bearish reversal. Alternatively, the Price creates a lower high, and the MACD creates higher lows, indicating a bullish reversal. MACD Divergence after a significant uptrend suggests that the buyers are losing power. MACD Divergence after a downtrend indicates that the sellers are losing control.

Entry:

Bullish Signal: Enter a long position when the MACD shows higher lows and Price shows lower highs in a downtrend. Confirm the reversal with Price action or other indicators.

Bearish Signal: Enter a short position when the MACD shows lower lows and Price shows higher highs after an uptrend. Confirm reversal with Price action or other indicators.

Stop Loss:

The stop loss should be based on the previous Swing Low/Swing High, ATR (Average True Range), or any other indicator.

Exit Rules:

Profit Target: Your profit target should be based on your risk - reward ratio. It could be a specific percentage gain or a resistance/support level.

Trailing Stop: You can trail stop - loss to maximize your profit and ride the total momentum as the price moves in your favor.

Risk Management:

Position Sizing: Determine the appropriate size based on your risk tolerance and account size. You should park only 5% of your Capital at a time.

Risk - Reward Ratio: Ensure that your potential profit is significantly greater than your potential loss for each trade. Keep your Risk - Reward ratio at least 1:2.

Example:

For a Bullish example, refer to the attached chart of AUBANK. MACD makes higher lows in a downward trend, and Price makes lower highs. This Divergence indicates that bears are losing strength, and there may be a bullish reversal. On 03rd Apr - 2024, the price breakout the previous swing high. We take entry (buy stock) at 605.00 with a stop loss at 553.00 (Previous Swing low/Support) and a Target of 710.00. The Risk: The reward is 1:2, and the target hit on 05thSep - 2024, with 17.35% profit on the deployed Capital.

10

MACD Histogram Strategy

The MACD Histogram indicator represents the difference between the MACD line and the signal line to identify changes in momentum. It is designed as an early warning sign for signal line crossovers, the most frequent MACD signals.

Entry:

Bullish Signal: Enter a long position when the MACD Histogram crosses above zero, indicating bullish momentum.

Bearish Signal: Enter a short position when the MACD Histogram crosses below zero, signaling bearish momentum.

Stop Loss:

Stop loss should be previous swing low/high, Support/Resistance, or any other indicator.

Exit Rules:

Profit Target: Your profit target should be based on your risk - reward ratio. It could be a specific percentage gain or the next Support/Resistance.

Trailing Stop: You can trail stop - loss to maximize your profit and ride the total momentum as the price moves in your favor.

Risk Management:

Position Sizing: Determine the appropriate size based on your risk tolerance and account size. You should park only 5% of your Capital at a time.

Risk - Reward Ratio: Ensure that your potential profit is significantly greater than your potential loss for each trade. Keep your Risk - Reward ratio at least 1:2.

Example:

For a Bullish example, refer to the attached chart of Bharat Forge. On Nov 15, 2023, the MACD Histogram crossed above 0 (zero), so we await Price action. On Nov 22, 2023, the Price breaks out of the previous swing high. We take entry (buy stock) at 1097.00 with a stop loss at 1002.00 (Previous Swing Low) and a Target of 1287.00 (R: R 1:2). The Risk: reward achieved is 1:2, and the Target was hit on Jan 09, 2024, with a 17.32% profit on deployed Capital.

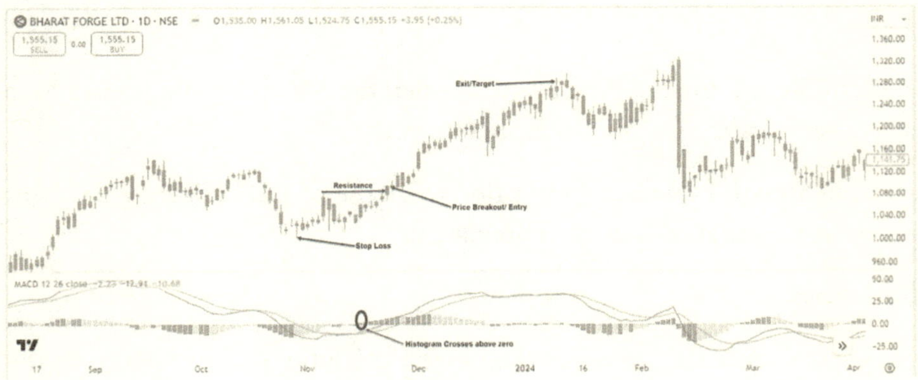

11

Combined MACD/RSI Signals

As MACD analyzes the trend and RSI identifies momentum, we can use combined MACD + RSI as a trading method that uses both indicators to analyze and trade the markets. Combining both momentum indicators may give more insight into what the market may do next and how it could move.

Entry:

Bullish Signal: Enter a long position when the MACD line (Blue line) crosses above the signal line (Red line) and the RSI moves upwards.

Bearish Signal: Enter a short position when the MACD line (Blue line) crosses below the signal line (Red line) and the RSI moves downwards.

Stop Loss:

Stop loss should be previous swing low/high, Support/Resistance, or any other indicator.

Exit Rules:

Profit Target: Your profit target should be based on your risk - reward ratio. It could be a specific percentage gain or the next Support/Resistance.

Trailing Stop: You can trail stop - loss to maximize your profit and ride the total momentum as the price moves in your favor.

Risk Management:

Position Sizing: Determine the appropriate size based on your risk tolerance and account size. You should park only 5% of your Capital at a time.

Risk - Reward Ratio: Ensure that your potential profit is significantly greater than your potential loss for each trade. Keep your Risk - Reward ratio at least 1:2.

Example:

For a Bullish example, refer to the attached chart of Aurobindo Pharma. On Nov 08 23, the MACD line (Blue line) crosses above the signal line (Red line), and the RSI is making a higher high. On the same day, the Price break out the previous swing high. We take entry (buy stock) at 937.00 with a stop loss at 834.00 (Previous Swing Low). Target of 1144.00 (R: R 1:2). The Risk: Reward achieved is 1:2, and Target hit on 15th Jan, 24 with 22.09% profit on deployed Capital.

12

Triple EMA/MACD Confluence

The confluence of multiple indicators can increase the probability of success. For example, we can use the confluence of the Triple EMA indicator with the MACD indicator for a sure shot.

Entry:

Bullish Signal: Enter a long position when the shortest length EMA (9 in our case) is moving/crosses above the mid length EMA (20 in our case) & Long length EMA (50 in our case), and MACD line (Blue line) is above signal line (Red line).

Bearish Signal: Enter a short position when the shortest length EMA (9 in our case) moves/crosses below the mid - length EMA (20 in our case) and the long - length EMA (50 in our case) and the MACD line (Blue line) is below the signal line (Red line).

Stop Loss:

Stop loss should be previous swing low/high, Support/Resistance, or any other indicator.

Exit Rules:

Profit Target: Your profit target should be based on your risk - reward ratio. It could be a specific percentage gain or the next Support/Resistance.

Trailing Stop: You can trail stop - loss to maximize your profit and ride the total momentum as the price moves in your favor.

Risk Management:

Position Sizing: Determine the appropriate size based on your risk tolerance and account size. You should park only 5% of your Capital at a time.

Risk - Reward Ratio: Ensure that your potential profit is significantly greater than your potential loss for each trade. Keep your Risk - Reward ratio at least 1:2.

Example:

For a Bullish example, refer to the attached chart of Axis Bank. On Nov 07 2023, the 9 EMA line crossed above the 20 & 50 EMA line. Also, the MACD line (Blue) is above the Signal line (Orange), and the Price traded above the previous swing high. We take entry (buy stock) at 1020.00 with a stop loss at 965.00 (Previous Swing Low). Target of 1130.00 (R: R 1:2). The Risk: Reward achieved is 1:2. Target hit on 05[th]Dec - 2023 with 10.78% profit on deployed Capital.

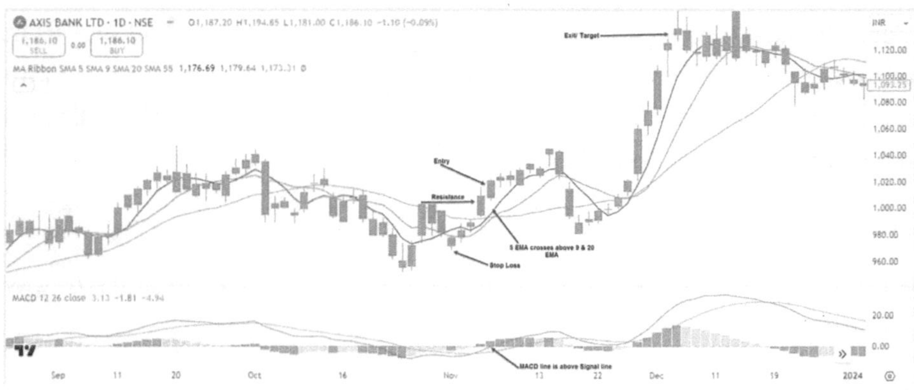

13

MACD Renko Entry Strategy

A Renko chart is a type of chart built using price movement rather than both Prices. When the Price moves in a specified amount, a new brick is formed, and each block is positioned at a 45 - degree angle (up or down) to the right of the prior brick. An up brick is typically colored green, while a down brick generally is colored red. We can use MACD on a RENKO chart for entry purposes.

Entry:

Bullish Signal: Enter a long position when the RENKO bricks are green, and the MACD line (Blue line) crosses above the signal line (Red line).

Bearish Signal: Enter a short position when the RENKO bricks are Red and the MACD line (Blue line) crosses below the signal line (Red line).

Stop Loss:

Stop loss should be previous swing low/high, Support/Resistance, or any other indicator.

Exit Rules:

Profit Target: Your profit target should be based on your risk - reward ratio. It could be a specific percentage gain or the next Support/Resistance.

Trailing Stop: You can trail stop - loss to maximize your profit and ride the total momentum as the price moves in your favor. You can also use green Renko bricks for trail purposes. One can exit when Red Renko bricks formed.

Risk Management:

Position Sizing: Determine the appropriate size based on your risk tolerance and account size. You should park only 5% of your Capital at a time.

Risk - Reward Ratio: Ensure that your potential profit is significantly greater than your potential loss for each trade. It would help if you kept your Risk - Reward ratio at least 1:2.

Example:

For a Bullish example, refer to the attached chart of Bajaj Finserv Ltd. On 26th Jul 2022, the MACD line crossed above the signal line, and Renko formed green bricks. We take entry (buy stock) at 1330.00 with a stop loss at 1260.00 (Previous Brick Low) and a Target of 1610.00 (R: R 1:2). The Risk: reward achieved is 1:4, and the Target hit on 22nd Aug - 2022 with 21.05% profit on deployed Capital.

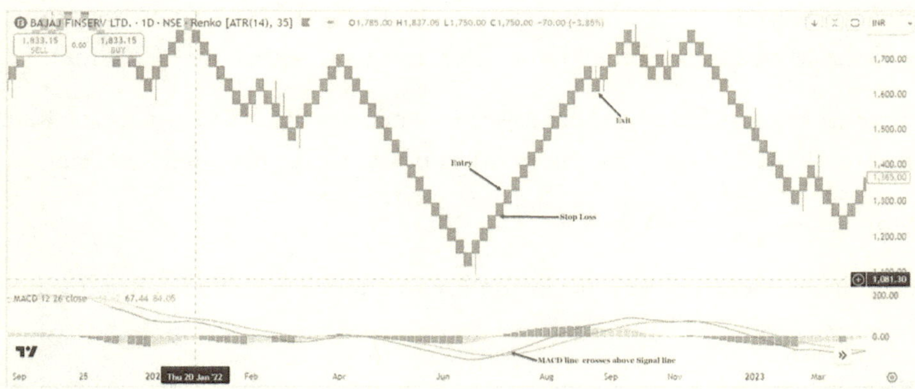

14

MACD/Stochastics/RSI Combo

Stochastic compares the asset's closing price to its Price over a certain period, while MACD shows two moving averages diverging and converging. RSI is the leading momentum indicator trader use to measure recent price changes. The confluence of multiple indicators can increase the probability of success. We can use the MACD, Stochastic, and RSI combo confluence for a sure shot.

Entry:

Bullish Signal:

Step 1: Look at stochastic, then make sure both K and D lines are in oversold regions.

Step 2: Use RSI to confirm the upward trend by ensuring it is above the middle line (50).

Step 3: Use the MACD to confirm the upward movement. Make sure the MACD line crosses above the signal line.

Step 4: Ensure that both stochastic lines have not hit overbought levels.

Step 5: Take a buy/long position.

Bearish Signal:

Step 1: First, look at stochastic, then ensure both K and D lines are in overbought regions.

Step 2: Use the RSI to confirm the downward trend, ensuring it is below the middle line (50).

Step 3: Use the MACD to confirm the downward movement. Make sure the MACD line crosses below the signal line.

Step 4: Ensure that both stochastic lines have not hit oversold levels.

Step 5: Take a sell/short position once all rules are met.

Stop Loss:

Stop loss should be based on previous swing low/high, support/resistance, or any other indicator.

Exit Rules:

Profit Target: Your profit target should be based on your risk - reward ratio. It could be a specific percentage gain or the next Support/Resistance.

Trailing Stop: You can trail stop - loss to maximize your profit and ride the total momentum as the price moves in your favor.

Risk Management:

Position Sizing: Determine the appropriate size based on your risk tolerance and account size. You should park only 5% of your Capital at a time.

Risk - Reward Ratio: Ensure that your potential profit is significantly greater than your potential loss for each trade. It would help if you kept your Risk - Reward ratio at least 1:2.

Example:

For a bullish example, refer to the attached chart for Balkrishna Industries. During the Feb - 2024 month, the stock was trading in the oversold zone as per the Stochastic indicator. On 21st Mar 2024, the RSI trades above 50, the MACD line is above the signal line, and the Stochastic is still below the Overbought zone. We take entry (buy stock) at 2310.00 with a stop loss at 2190.00 (Previous Swing Low) and a Target of 2550.00 (R: R 1:2). The Risk: Reward achieved is 1:2, and the Target hit on 16[th]May 2024 with 10.39% profit on deployed Capital.

RSI Riches

The Relative Strength Index (RSI) is a must-know indicator for any trader. This chapter simplifies RSI strategies, focusing on actionable setups. The RSI Overbought/Oversold strategy identifies potential reversal points when the RSI reaches extreme levels. The RSI/Price Divergence Strategy helps you detect hidden opportunities by comparing price action with RSI behavior. Breakout traders will benefit from the RSI Trendline Breakouts, which pinpoint momentum bursts. The Heikin-Ashi/RSI Smoothing strategy reduces market noise and clarifies trends, while the RSI/OBV Confirmation strategy combines RSI with On-Balance Volume for additional validation. By the end of this chapter, you'll understand how to harness RSI to spot trading opportunities and avoid false signals.

15

RSI Overbought/Oversold

The Relative Strength Index (RSI) is a popular momentum oscillator used to identify overbought and oversold zones of market/stock. Generally, an RSI>70 is considered an overbought zone (Considering a selling opportunity) & RSI<30 is regarded as an oversold zone (Considering a buying opportunity).

Entry:

Bullish Signal: Look for a buying opportunity when the RSI crosses below 30 and moves back above 30. To avoid false signals, use additional indicators such as moving averages, MACD, or price action (previous swing high breakout).

Bearish Signal: When the RSI crosses above 70 and then moves back below 70, one can look for a selling opportunity. To avoid false signals, one can use additional indicators such as moving averages, MACD, or price action (previous swing low breakdown).

Stop Loss:

Stop loss should be based on previous swing low/high, support/resistance, or any other indicator.

Exit Rules:

Profit Target: Your profit target should be based on your risk - reward ratio. It could be a specific percentage gain or the next Support/Resistance.

Trailing Stop: You can trail stop - loss to maximize your profit and ride the total momentum as the price moves in your favor.

Risk Management:

Position Sizing: Determine the appropriate size based on your risk tolerance and account size. You should park only 5% of your Capital at a time.

Risk - Reward Ratio: Ensure that your potential profit is significantly greater than your potential loss for each trade. It would help if you kept your Risk - Reward ratio at least 1:2.

Example:

For a Bullish example, refer to the attached chart of the Bank of India. On 27th Feb 2023, the RSI of the stock was below 30, i.e., in the oversold zone. On 28th Feb 2023, the RSI reflected and closed above 30, showing a bullish reversal. We are waiting for price action; on 01st Mar - 2023, the stock price will break out of the previous swing high. We take entry (buy stock) at 74.00 with a stop loss at 66.00 (Previous Swing Low) and a Target of 90.00 (R: R 1:2). The Risk: Reward achieved is 1:2, and Target hit on 16thAug - 2023 with 21.62% profit on deployed Capital.

16

RSI/Price Divergence Strategy

RSI (Relative Strength Index) is a momentum oscillator that measures the speed and change of price movements. Normally, Price and RSI move in the same direction, i.e., the trend direction. RSI divergence occurs when Price and RSI start moving in opposite directions. RSI divergence indicates potential for trend change.

Entry:

Bullish Signal: After following a downward/bearish trend, the Price still makes Lower highs, but the RSI starts making higher lows. To avoid false signals, one can use additional indicators such as moving averages, MACD, or price action (previous swing high breakout).

Bearish Signal: After following an upward/bullish trend, the Price still makes higher lows, but the RSI makes lower highs. To avoid false signals, one can use additional indicators such as moving averages, MACD, or price action (previous swing high breakout).

Stop Loss:

Stop loss should be based on previous swing low/high, support/resistance, or any other indicator.

Exit Rules:

Profit Target: Your profit target should be based on your risk - reward ratio. It could be a specific percentage gain or the next Support/Resistance.

Trailing Stop: You can trail stop - loss to maximize your profit and ride the total momentum as the price moves in your favor.

Risk Management:

Position Sizing: Determine the appropriate size based on your risk tolerance and account size. You should park only 5% of your Capital at a time.

Risk - Reward Ratio: Ensure that your potential profit is significantly greater than your potential loss for each trade. It would help if you kept your Risk - Reward ratio at least 1:2.

Example:

For a Bullish example, refer to the attached chart of Bharat Dynamics. The stock was in a downtrend; now, the Price is still making lower highs, whereas the RSI is starting to make higher lows (indicated with blue lines). On 13th Nov 2023, the Price breaks out of the previous swing high. We take entry (buy stock) at 540.00 with a stop loss at 450.00 (Previous Swing Low) and a Target of 720.00 (R: R 1:2). The Risk: Reward achieved is 1:2, and Target hit on 18th Dec - 2023 with 33.33% profit on deployed Capital.

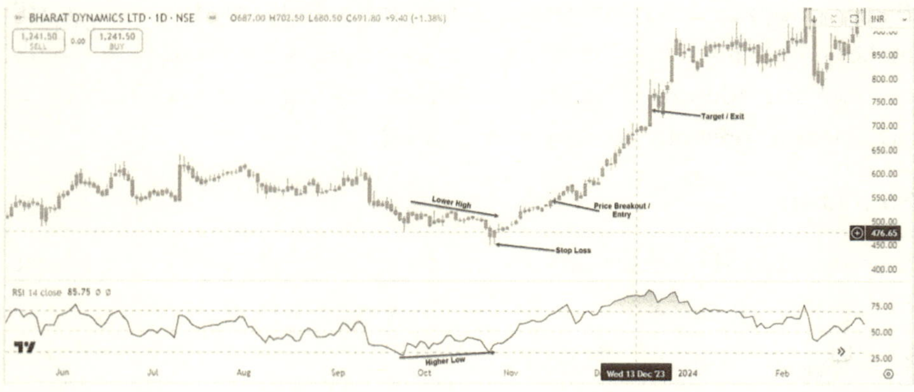

17

RSI Trendline Breakouts Strategy

RSI (Relative Strength Index) is a momentum oscillator that measures the speed and change of price movements. Similar to Price, you can draw a trend line on RSI. One can trade a breakout/breakdown of the RSI trend line.

Entry:

Bullish Signal: When the RSI is downtrend, draw a trend line by connecting its highs. When the RSI breaks this trend line, buy the script. You can use additional indicators such as moving averages, MACD, or price action (previous swing high breakout) can be used to avoid false signals.

Bearish Signal: When the RSI is uptrend, draw a trend line by connecting its lows. When the RSI breaks this trend line, sell the script. To avoid false signals, one can use additional indicators such as moving averages, MACD, or price action (previous swing low breakdown).

Stop Loss:

Stop loss should be based on previous swing low/high, support/resistance, or any other indicator.

Exit Rules:

Profit Target: Your profit target should be based on your risk - reward ratio. It could be a specific percentage gain or the next Support/Resistance.

Trailing Stop: You can trail stop - loss to maximize your profit and ride the total momentum as the price moves in your favor.

Risk Management:

Position Sizing: Determine the appropriate size based on your risk tolerance and account size. You should park only 5% of your Capital at a time.

Risk - Reward Ratio: Ensure that your potential profit is significantly greater than your potential loss for each trade. It would help if you kept your Risk - Reward ratio at least 1:2.

Example:

For a bullish example, refer to the attached chart for Bharat Electronics. RSI was in a downtrend. Therefore, a trend line is marked by connecting highs of RSI (Blue line). On 19th Feb 2024, the RSI breaks out its trend line, and we wait for price action, i.e., a breakout of the previous swing high. On 23rd Feb 2024, the Price broke out of the last high swing. We take entry (buy stock) at 197.00 with a stop loss at 171.00 (Previous Swing Low) and a Target of 250.00 (R: R 1:2). The Risk: Reward achieved is 1:2, and Target hit on 18[th]May - 2024 with 26.90% profit on deployed Capital.

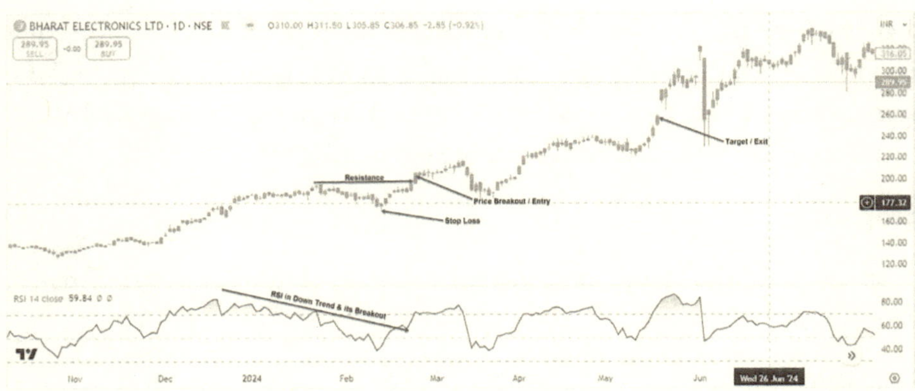

18

Heikin - Ashi and RSI Smoothing Strategy

Heikin - Ashi is a type of candlestick chart that helps to filter out market noise. In contrast, RSI is a momentum oscillator that measures the speed and change of price movements. Smoothing RSI involves applying an additional moving average to reduce noise and false signals. The idea is that we combine all three to get a more probable trade in our favor.

Entry:

Bullish Signal: We take a bullish entry when the Hekin - Ashi candle is green without any lower wick and the RSI is trending above 50 and 5 MA.

Bearish Signal: When the Hekin - Ashi candle is red without an upper wick, the RSI is trending below 50, and 5MA; we take a bearish entry.

Stop Loss:

The stop loss should be the previous swing low/high or the formation of 2 consecutive candles, i.e., 2 Red candles if we are bullish and 2 Green candles if we are bearish.

Exit Rules:

Profit Target: Your profit target should be based on your risk - reward ratio. It could be a specific percentage gain or the next Support/Resistance.

Trailing Stop: You can trail stop - loss to maximize your profit and ride the total momentum as the price moves in your favor.

Risk Management:

Position Sizing: Determine the appropriate size based on your risk tolerance and account size. You should park only 5% of your Capital at a time.

Risk - Reward Ratio: Ensure that your potential profit is significantly greater than your potential loss for each trade. It would help if you kept your Risk - Reward ratio at least 1:2.

Example:

For a Bullish example, refer to the attached chart of BHEL. After 9 continuous red Heikin Ashi candles, a green Hekin Ashi candle formed on 21st Mar 2021. RSI is trading at 51.37, i.e., above 50 and 5 DMA. We take entry (buy stock) at 234.00 with a stop loss at 207.00 (Previous Swing Low) and a Target of 290.00 (R: R 1:2). The Risk: reward achieved is 1:2, and the Target hit on 02nd May 2024 with 23.93% profit on deployed Capital.

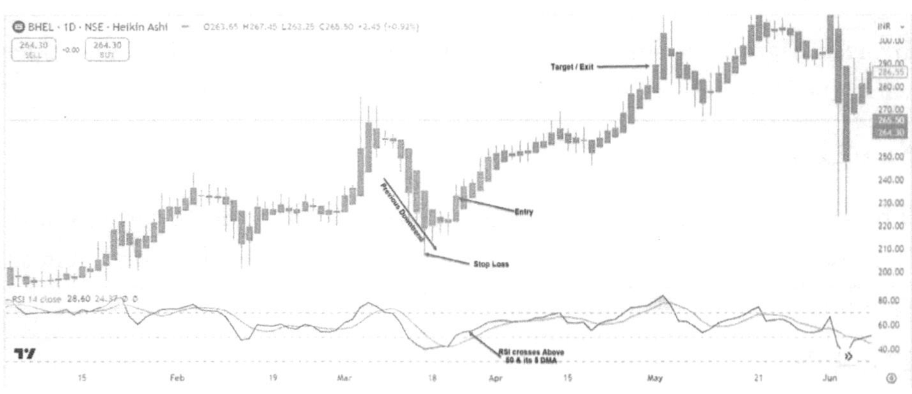

19

RSI/OBV Confirmation Strategy

RSI is a momentum oscillator that measures the speed and change of price movements. It ranges from 0 to 100, with levels above 70 indicating overbought conditions and below 30 indicating oversold conditions. OBV is a volume - based indicator that combines Price and volume to show the flow of money into and out of a stock. It helps to confirm the strength of price movements.

Entry:

Bullish Signal: Look for a buy signal when the RSI moves above 30 and the OBV rises simultaneously. This confirms that momentum and volume support the price movement.

Bearish Signal: Look for a sell signal when the RSI moves below 70 and the OBV declines simultaneously. This confirms that momentum and volume support the negative price movement.

Stop Loss:

Stop loss should be based on previous swing low/high, support/resistance, or any other indicator.

Exit Rules:

Profit Target: Your profit target should be based on your risk - reward ratio. It could be a specific percentage gain or the next Support/Resistance.

Trailing Stop: You can trail stop - loss to maximize your profit and ride the total momentum as the price moves in your favor.

Risk Management:

Position Sizing: Determine the appropriate size based on your risk tolerance and account size. You should park only 5% of your Capital at a time.

Risk - Reward Ratio: Ensure that your potential profit is significantly greater than your potential loss for each trade. It would help if you kept your Risk - Reward ratio at least 1:2.

Example:

For a Bullish example, refer to the attached chart of Berger Paints. On 28th Feb - 2023, the Price breaks out of the previous swing high, RSI is moving upward continuously above 30, and OBV is increasing day by day & also breaks out of its last swing high. We take entry (buy stock) at 483.00 with a stop loss at 439.00 (Previous Swing Low) and a Target of 571.00 (R: R 1:2). The Risk: Reward achieved is 1:2, and Target hit on 21st Jun - 2023 with 18.22% profit on deployed Capital.

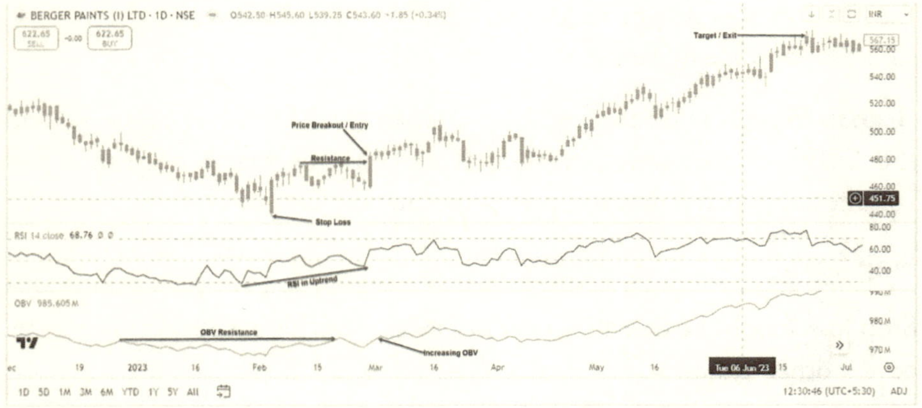

Stochastics Setups

Stochastics is a momentum indicator that excels at identifying overbought and oversold conditions. This chapter introduces five beginner-friendly stochastic strategies. Start with the Stochastics Crossover, which signals potential trend changes when %K crosses %D. The Stochastics Divergence strategy reveals early reversal opportunities by comparing price and indicator behavior. Advanced setups include Stochastics/RSI Double Smooth, which combines two momentum tools for cleaner signals, and Stochastics Momentum Index (SMI) for refined trend analysis. Finally, the Stochastics Rainbow Strategy employs multiple stochastic lines for a broader view of market momentum. With clear explanations and actionable steps, you'll gain confidence in timing your trades and improving your win rate.

20

Stochastics Crossover Strategy

A Stochastic Oscillator is a momentum indicator that compares a security's closing price to a range of its prices over a certain period. It consists of the %K line (the main line) and the %D line (the signal line), a moving average of the %K line.

Entry:

Bullish Signal: Bullish Crossover occurs when the %K line crosses above the %D line, especially from below the 20 (Oversold level). This bullish crossover indicates a potential buy signal.

Bearish Signal: Bearish Crossover occurs when the %K line crosses below the %D line, especially from above the 80 (Overbought level). This bearish crossover indicates a potential sell signal.

Stop Loss:

Stop loss should be based on previous swing low/high, support/resistance, or any other indicator.

Exit Rules:

Profit Target: Your profit target should be based on your risk - reward ratio. It could be a specific percentage gain or the next Support/Resistance.

Trailing Stop: You can trail stop - loss to maximize your profit and ride the total momentum as the price moves in your favor.

Risk Management:

Position Sizing: Determine the appropriate size based on your risk tolerance and account size. You should park only 5% of your Capital at a time.

Risk - Reward Ratio: Ensure that your potential profit is significantly greater than your potential loss for each trade. It would help if you kept your Risk - Reward ratio at least 1:2.

Example:

For a Bullish example, refer to the attached chart of Bharat Forge. On 26[th]Mar - 2024, the Stochastics %K line crossed above the %D line & 20. We are waiting for price action. On 01st Apr - 2024, the Price broke out its previous swing high. We take entry (buy stock) at 1150.00 with a stop loss at 1085.00 (Previous Swing Low) and a Target of 1280.00 (R: R 1:2). The Risk: reward achieved is 1:2, and the Target hit on 25th Apr - 2024 with 11.30% profit on deployed Capital.

21

Stochastic Oscillator Divergence Strategy

The Stochastic Oscillator is used to identify potential trend reversals and overbought/oversold conditions. A Stochastic Indicator value of 20 or less indicates that the market is oversold, and a value of 80 or above indicates that the market is overbought.

Bullish Divergence occurs when the Price makes a lower low and the Stochastic makes a higher low simultaneously. Bearish Divergence occurs when the Price makes a higher high, and the Stochastic makes a lower high simultaneously.

Entry:

Bullish Signal: Enter a long position when the Stochastic is in the oversold zone, i.e., below 20. Price makes a lower low, and Stochastic makes a higher low simultaneously. There is price action, i.e., a break out of the previous swing high/resistance.

Bearish Signal: Enter a short position when the Stochastic is in the overbought zone, i.e., above 80. Price makes a higher high, and Stochastic makes a lower high simultaneously. There is price action, i.e., a breakdown of the previous swing low/support.

Stop Loss:

The stop loss should be based on the previous Swing Low/Swing High, ATR (Average True Range), or any other indicator.

Exit Rules:

Profit Target: Your profit target should be based on your risk - reward ratio. It could be a specific percentage gain or a resistance/support level.

Trailing Stop: You can trail stop - loss to maximize your profit and ride the total momentum as the price moves in your favor.

Risk Management:

Position Sizing: Determine the appropriate size based on your risk tolerance and account size. You should park only 5% of your Capital at a time.

Risk - Reward Ratio: Ensure that your potential profit is significantly greater than your potential loss for each trade. It would help if you kept your Risk - Reward ratio at least 1:2.

Example:

For a Bullish example, refer to the attached chart of Adani Power. On 27th Oct 23, Stochastic was below 20, i.e., in the oversold zone; Stochastic was making a higher low, the Price was making a lower low, and the Green candle broke the previous swing high of 346.70. We take entry (buy stock) at 350.00 with a stop loss of 285.00 (Previous Swing low/Support) and Target of 500.00 (1:2). The Risk: Reward achieved is almost 1:2.3 and Target hit on Dec 05, 23 with 42.86% profit on deployed Capital.

22

Stochastics/RSI Double Smooth Strategy

The Stochastics/RSI Double Smooth strategy combines two popular technical indicators:

Stochastic Oscillator: Measures momentum by comparing the closing price to its price range over a specific period.

Relative Strength Index (RSI): Measures the speed and change of price movements.

Both indicators are smoothed twice to reduce noise and false signals.

Entry:

Bullish Signal: Enter a long position when the smoothed RSI is above 50 and the smoothed %K line crosses above the smoothed %D line.

Bearish Signal: Enter a short position when the smoothed RSI is below 50 and the smoothed %K line crosses below the smoothed %D line.

Stop Loss:

The stop loss should be based on the previous Swing Low/Swing High, ATR (Average True Range), or any other indicator.

Exit Rules:

Profit Target: Your profit target should be based on your risk - reward ratio. It could be a specific percentage gain or a resistance/support level.

Trailing Stop: You can trail stop - loss to maximize your profit and ride the total momentum as the price moves in your favor.

Risk Management:

Position Sizing: Determine the appropriate size based on your risk tolerance and account size. You should park only 5% of your Capital at a time.

Risk - Reward Ratio: Ensure that your potential profit is significantly greater than your potential loss for each trade. It would help if you kept your Risk - Reward ratio at least 1:2.

Example:

For a Bullish example, refer to the attached chart of AEGIS Logistics Ltd. On Mar28, 2024, RSI crossed above 50 &Smoothed SMA on Apr 09, 2024, %K of Stochastic crosses above %D & smoothed %K. On Apr 10, 2024, the Price breaks out of the previous swing high. We take entry (buy stock) at 465.00 with a stop loss of 355.00 (Previous Swing low/Support) and a Target of 685.00 (1:2). The Risk: Reward achieved is 1:2 and Target hit on Apr29, 2024, with 47.31% profit on deployed Capital.

23

Stochastics Momentum Index (SMI) Strategy

The Stochastic Momentum Index (SMI) is a technical indicator that helps traders identify potential trend reversals and overbought/oversold conditions. It's an advanced version of the Stochastic Oscillator, providing smoother signals. SMI oscillates between +100 and- 100; values above +40 indicate overbought conditions, and Values below- 40 indicate oversold conditions. The zero line acts as a signal line.

Entry:

Bullish Signal: Enter a long position when the SMI crosses above the- 40 line from below.

Bearish Signal: Enter a short position when the SMI crosses below the +40 line from above.

Stop Loss:

The stop loss should be based on the previous Swing Low/Swing High, ATR (Average True Range), or any other indicator.

Exit Rules:

Profit Target: Your profit target should be based on your risk - reward ratio. It could be a specific percentage gain or a resistance/support level.

Trailing Stop: You can trail stop - loss to maximize your profit and ride the total momentum as the price moves in your favor.

Risk Management:

Position Sizing: Determine the appropriate size based on your risk tolerance and account size. You should park only 5% of your Capital at a time.

Risk - Reward Ratio: Ensure that your potential profit is significantly greater than your potential loss for each trade. It would help if you kept your Risk - Reward ratio at least 1:2.

Example:

For a Bullish example, refer to the attached chart of AETHER Industries Ltd. On Mar 27, 2024, SMI crosses above- 40. On Apr 03, 2024, the Price breaks out of the previous swing high. We take entry (buy stock) at 825.00 with a stop loss of 760.00 (Previous Swing low/Support) and Target of 960.00 (1:2). The Risk: Reward achieved is 1:2 and Target hit on Jun 28, 2024, with 16.36% profit on deployed Capital.

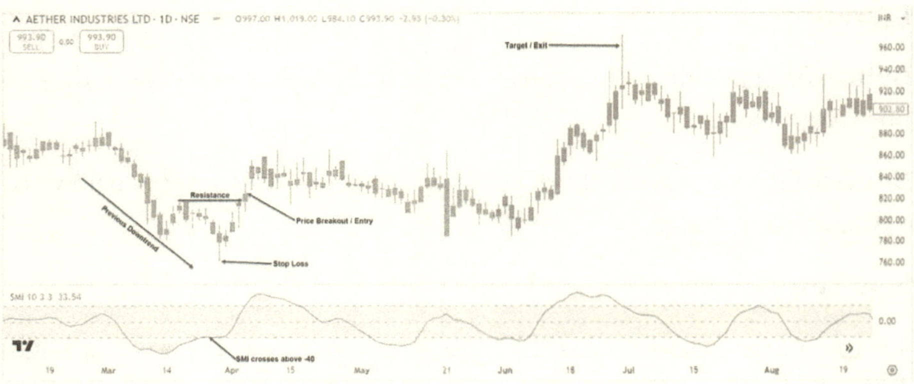

24

Stochastics Rainbow Strategy

The Stochastic Rainbow Strategy is a technical analysis tool that combines multiple moving averages with the Stochastic Oscillator to identify potential trend changes and trading opportunities. This strategy benefits beginners as it visually represents market trends and momentum. We'll use three exponential moving averages (EMAs) with different periods: Short - term EMA (5 periods), Medium - term EMA (10 periods) & Long - term EMA (20 periods). Stochastic oscillator indicator compares the closing price to its price range over a specific period.

Entry:

Bullish Signal: Enter a long position when the Short - term EMA > Medium - term EMA > Long - term EMA and Stochastic Oscillator crosses above the 30 from below.

Bearish Signal: Enter a short position when the Long - term EMA > Medium - term EMA > Short - term EMA and Stochastic Oscillator crosses below 80 from above.

Stop Loss:

The stop loss should be based on the previous Swing Low/Swing High, ATR (Average True Range), or any other indicator.

Exit Rules:

Profit Target: Your profit target should be based on your risk - reward ratio. It could be a specific percentage gain or a resistance/support level.

Trailing Stop: You can trail stop - loss to maximize your profit and ride the total momentum as the price moves in your favor.

Risk Management:

Position Sizing: Determine the appropriate size based on your risk tolerance and account size. You should park only 5% of your Capital at a time.

Risk - Reward Ratio: Ensure that your potential profit is significantly greater than your potential loss for each trade. It would help if you kept your Risk - Reward ratio at least 1:2.

Example:

For a Bullish example, refer to the attached AFFLE (I) Ltd chart. On Apr 26, 2024, the Stochastic oscillator shows an uptrend and 5EMA>10EMA>20EMA.We take entry (buy stock) at 1105.00 with a stop loss of 1030.00 (Previous Swing low/Support) and Target of 1260.00 (1:2). The Risk: reward achieved is 1:2, and the Target was hit on May 27, 2024, with a 14.03% profit on deployed Capital.

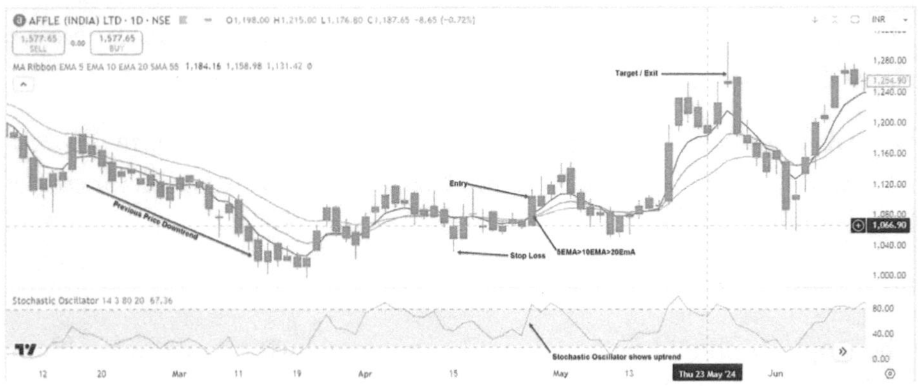

Ichimoku Clouds

The Ichimoku Cloud is a comprehensive trading system that might seem complex but offers incredible clarity once understood. This chapter breaks it down into six strategies. The Ichimoku Cloud Breakout highlights major trend changes when price breaks above or below the cloud. The Ichimoku Leading Span Breakout focuses on future projections to anticipate price action. Ichimoku & Candlestick Confluence merges candlestick patterns with the cloud for precise entries. Learn to spot trend reversals with Kumo Twists and Rotation, and use Lagging Span Mean Reversions for additional confirmation. Finally, the Ichimoku & Renko Combo integrates Renko charts for a simplified view of trends. Beginners will learn to use this powerful tool to identify trends, support, resistance, and reversals with ease.

25

Ichimoku Cloud Breakout Strategy

The Ichimoku Cloud, also known as Ichimoku Kinko Hyo, is a versatile indicator that defines support and resistance, identifies trend direction, gauges momentum, and provides trading signals. Developed by Goichi Hosoda, a Japanese journalist, in the late 1960s, the Ichimoku Cloud has gained popularity among traders worldwide. The Ichimoku Cloud consists of five lines: Tenkan - sen (Conversion Line), Kijun - sen (Base Line), Senkou Span A (Leading Span A), Senkou Span B (Leading Span B) & Chikou Span (Lagging Span). The area between Senkou Span A and B is the "Kumo" or "Cloud."

Entry:

Bullish Signal: Enter a long position when the Price breaks above the cloud.

Bearish Signal: Enter a short position when the Price breaks below the cloud.

Stop Loss:

The stop loss should be based on the previous Swing Low/Swing High, ATR (Average True Range), or any other indicator.

Exit Rules:

Profit Target: Your profit target should be based on your risk - reward ratio. It could be a specific percentage gain or a resistance/support level.

Trailing Stop: You can trail stop - loss to maximize your profit and ride the total momentum as the price moves in your favor.

Risk Management:

Position Sizing: Determine the appropriate size based on your risk tolerance and account size. You should park only 5% of your Capital at a time.

Risk - Reward Ratio: Ensure that your potential profit is significantly greater than your potential loss for each trade. It would help if you kept your Risk - Reward ratio at least 1:2.

Example:

For a Bullish example, refer to the attached chart of ABCAPITAL. On Jan 11, 2024, the Price crosses above Ichimoku Cloud. We take entry (buy stock) at 180.00 with a stop loss of 155.00 (Previous Swing low/Support) and a Target of 230.00 (1:2). The Risk: reward achieved is 1:2, and the Target was hit on Apr 25, 2024, with 27.78% profit on deployed Capital.

26

Ichimoku Leading Span Breakout Strategy

The Ichimoku Cloud, also known as Ichimoku Kinko Hyo, is a versatile indicator that defines support and resistance, identifies trend direction, gauges momentum, and provides trading signals. Developed by Goichi Hosoda, a Japanese journalist, in the late 1960s, the Ichimoku Cloud has gained popularity among traders worldwide. The Ichimoku Cloud consists of five lines: Tenkan - sen (Conversion Line), Kijun - sen (Base Line), Senkou Span A (Leading Span A), Senkou Span B (Leading Span B) & Chikou Span (Lagging Span). The area between Senkou Span A and B is the "Kumo" or "Cloud."

Entry:

Bullish Signal: Enter a long position when the Closing Price is above the Leading Span A.

Bearish Signal: Enter a short position when the Closing Price is below the Leading Span A.

Stop Loss:

The stop loss should be based on the previous Swing Low/Swing High, ATR (Average True Range), or any other indicator.

Exit Rules:

Profit Target: Your profit target should be based on your risk - reward ratio. It could be a specific percentage gain or a resistance/support level.

Trailing Stop: You can trail stop - loss to maximize your profit and ride the total momentum as the price moves in your favor.

Risk Management:

Position Sizing: Determine the appropriate size based on your risk tolerance and account size. You should park only 5% of your Capital at a time.

Risk - Reward Ratio: Ensure that your potential profit is significantly greater than your potential loss for each trade. It would help if you kept your Risk - Reward ratio at least 1:2.

Example:

For a Bullish example, refer to the attached chart of HAPPIEST MINDS TECH. On Jun 06, 2024, the closing price (820.55) is above Ichimoku Leading Span A (804.64). We take entry (buy stock) at 820.00 with a stop loss of 760.00 (Previous Swing low/Support) and a Target of 940.00 (1:2). The Risk: Reward achieved is 1:2 and Target hit on Jun 21, 2024, with 14.63% profit on deployed Capital.

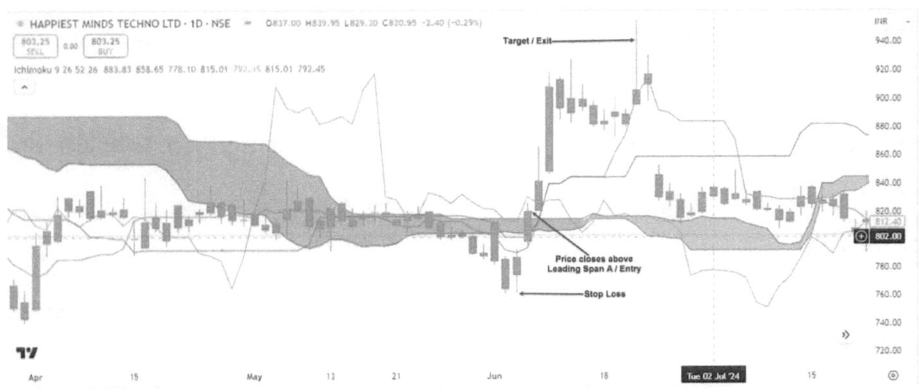

27

Ichimoku & Candlestick Confluence Strategy

The Ichimoku Cloud, also known as Ichimoku Kinko Hyo, is a versatile indicator that defines support and resistance, identifies trend direction, gauges momentum, and provides trading signals. Developed by Goichi Hosoda, a Japanese journalist, in the late 1960s, the Ichimoku Cloud has gained popularity among traders worldwide. The Ichimoku Cloud consists of five lines: Tenkan - sen (Conversion Line), Kijun - sen (Base Line), Senkou Span A (Leading Span A), Senkou Span B (Leading Span B) & Chikou Span (Lagging Span). The area between Senkou Span A and B is the "Kumo" or "Cloud."

This strategy looks for confluence between the Ichimoku Cloud and candlestick patterns. Here's how it works: Identify the overall trend using the Ichimoku Cloud. Look for candlestick patterns that align with the trend. Use additional Ichimoku components for confirmation.

Entry:

Bullish Signal: Enter a long position when the Closing Price breaks above the cloud and the Tenkan - sen crosses above the Kijun - sen (Base Line).

Bearish Signal: Enter a short position when the Closing Price breaks below the cloud and the Tenkan - sen crosses below the Kijun - sen (Base Line).

Stop Loss:

The stop loss should be based on the previous Swing Low/Swing High, ATR (Average True Range), or any other indicator.

Exit Rules:

Profit Target: Your profit target should be based on your risk - reward ratio. It could be a specific percentage gain or a resistance/support level.

Trailing Stop: You can trail stop - loss to maximize your profit and ride the total momentum as the price moves in your favor.

Risk Management:

Position Sizing: Determine the appropriate size based on your risk tolerance and account size. You should park only 5% of your Capital at a time.

Risk - Reward Ratio: Ensure that your potential profit is significantly greater than your potential loss for each trade. It would help if you kept your Risk - Reward ratio at least 1:2.

Example:

For a Bullish example, refer to the attached AFFLE (I) Ltd chart. On May 17, 2024, the closing price crossed above the Ichimoku Cloud, and the Tenkan - sen (Dark Blue line) crossed above the Kijun - sen (Dark Red line). We took entry (buy stock) at 1175.00 with a stop loss of 1050.00 (Previous Swing low/Support) and a Target of 1425.00 (1:2). The Risk: reward achieved is 1:2, and the Target was hit on Jul 08, 2024, with 21.28% profit on deployed Capital.

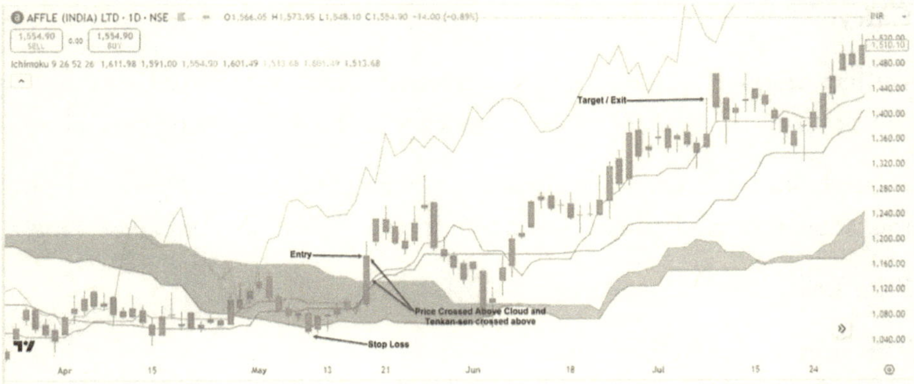

28

Kumo Twists and Rotation Strategy

The Ichimoku Cloud is a technical indicator showing support and resistance levels, trend direction, and strength. Kumo is the "cloud" part of the Ichimoku Cloud, formed between two lines (Senkou Span A and Senkou Span B).The Kumo twist occurs when the two lines form the Kumo cross, changing the cloud's color. Kumo Rotation refers to the change in direction of the Kumo (from flat to angled up or down).

Entry:

Bullish Signal: Enter a long position when the price breaks above the Kumo after a bullish twist and rotation.

Bearish Signal: Enter a short position when the price breaks below the Kumo after a bearish twist and rotation.

Stop Loss:

The stop loss should be based on the previous Swing Low/Swing High, ATR (Average True Range), or any other indicator.

Exit Rules:

Profit Target: Your profit target should be based on your risk - reward ratio. It could be a specific percentage gain or a resistance/support level.

Trailing Stop: You can trail stop - loss to maximize your profit and ride the total momentum as the price moves in your favor.

Risk Management:

Position Sizing: Determine the appropriate size based on your risk tolerance and account size. You should park only 5% of your Capital at a time.

Risk - Reward Ratio: Ensure that your potential profit is significantly greater than your potential loss for each trade. It would help if you kept your Risk - Reward ratio at least 1:2.

Example:

For a Bullish example, refer to the attached chart of ALKEM LAB. On Jun 20, 2024, a Kumo twist happens, and the direction of Kumo becomes upward, showing the change in direction. On Jul 08, 2024, the Price crossed above Kumo. Also, the Tenkan - sen line is trading above the Kijun - sen line. We take entry (buy stock) at 5225.00 with a stop loss of 4870.00 (Previous Swing low/Support) and Target of 5940.00 (1:2). The Risk: Reward achieved is 1:2 and Target hit on Aug 27 2024 with 13.68% profit on deployed Capital.

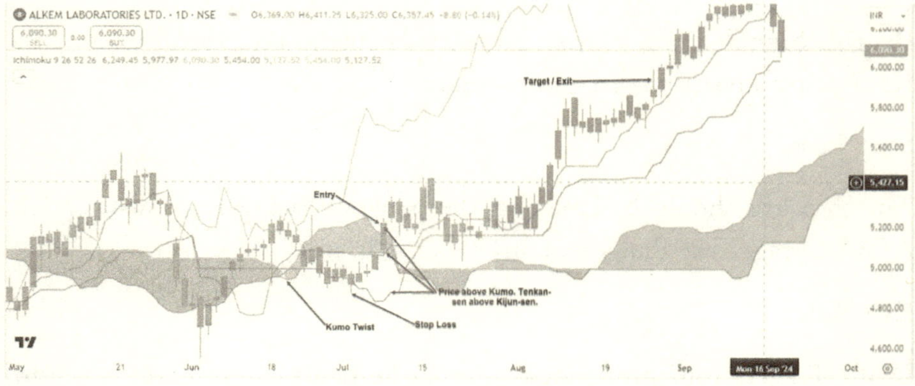

29

Lagging Span Mean Reversions

This strategy will focus on the Lagging Span (Chikou Span). Look for instances where the Lagging Span has deviated significantly from the Price. Ensure the Price is above the Ichimoku Cloud for uptrends. The Lagging Span should cross/above the Price. Tenkan - sen should cross/above Kijun - sen.

Entry:

Bullish Signal: Enter a long position when the Lagging Span crosses above the Price.

Bearish Signal: Enter a short position when the Lagging Span crosses below the Price.

Stop Loss:

The stop loss should be based on the previous Swing Low/Swing High, ATR (Average True Range), or any other indicator.

Exit Rules:

Profit Target: Your profit target should be based on your risk - reward ratio. It could be a specific percentage gain or a resistance/support level.

Trailing Stop: You can trail stop - loss to maximize your profit and ride the total momentum as the price moves in your favor.

Risk Management:

Position Sizing: Determine the appropriate size based on your risk tolerance and account size. You should park only 5% of your Capital at a time.

Risk - Reward Ratio: Ensure that your potential profit is significantly greater than your potential loss for each trade. It would help if you kept your Risk - Reward ratio at least 1:2.

Example:

For a Bullish example, refer to the attached chart of ANGELONE. On Jun 05, 2023, Lagging was trading far above Price, Price was trading above Kumo & Conversion line, and Conversion line was trading above Baseline. We take entry (buy stock) at 1380.00 with a stop loss of 1180.00 (Previous Swing low/Support) and Target of 1780.00 (1:2). The Risk: Reward achieved is 1:2 and Target hit on Jul 04 2023 with 29.00% profit on deployed Capital.

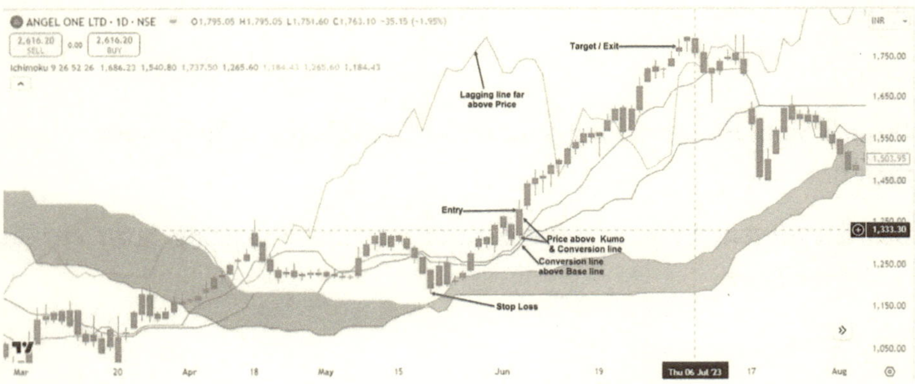

30

Ichimoku & Renko Combo Strategy

The Ichimoku Cloud, also known as Ichimoku Kinko Hyo, is a versatile indicator that defines support and resistance, identifies trend direction, gauges momentum, and provides trading signals. Developed by Goichi Hosoda, a Japanese journalist, in the late 1960s, the Ichimoku Cloud has gained popularity among traders worldwide. The Ichimoku Cloud consists of five lines: Tenkan - sen (Conversion Line), Kijun - sen (Base Line), Senkou Span A (Leading Span A), Senkou Span B (Leading Span B) & Chikou Span (Lagging Span). The area between Senkou Span A and B is the "Kumo" or "Cloud."

Renko Charts are based on price movement, not time. Renko filter noise and sideways movement. Each brick represents a fixed price movement.

Entry:

Bullish Signal: Enter a long position when the Price breaks above the cloud, Tenkan - sen crosses/trades above Kijun - sen, and a green Renko brick forms above the cloud.

Bearish Signal: Enter a short position when the Price breaks below the cloud, Tenkan - sen crosses/trades below Kijun - sen, and a red Renko brick forms below the cloud.

Stop Loss:

The stop loss should be based on the previous Swing Low/Swing High, ATR (Average True Range), or any other indicator.

Exit Rules:

Profit Target: Your profit target should be based on your risk - reward ratio. It could be a specific percentage gain or a resistance/support level.

Trailing Stop: You can trail stop - loss to maximize your profit and ride the total momentum as the price moves in your favor.

Risk Management:

Position Sizing: Determine the appropriate size based on your risk tolerance and account size. You should park only 5% of your Capital at a time.

Risk - Reward Ratio: Ensure that your potential profit is significantly greater than your potential loss for each trade. It would help if you kept your Risk - Reward ratio at least 1:2.

Example:

For a Bullish example, refer to the attached chart of Alembic Pharma Ltd. On Jan 02, 2024, the Green Renko candle crosses above Ichimoku Cloud, and Tenkan - sen trades above Kijun - sen. We take entry (buy stock) at 780.00 with a stop loss of 710.00 (Previous Swing low/Support) and Target of 920.00 (1:2). The Risk: reward achieved is 1:2, and the Target was hit on Jan 15, 2024, with 17.95% profit on deployed Capital.

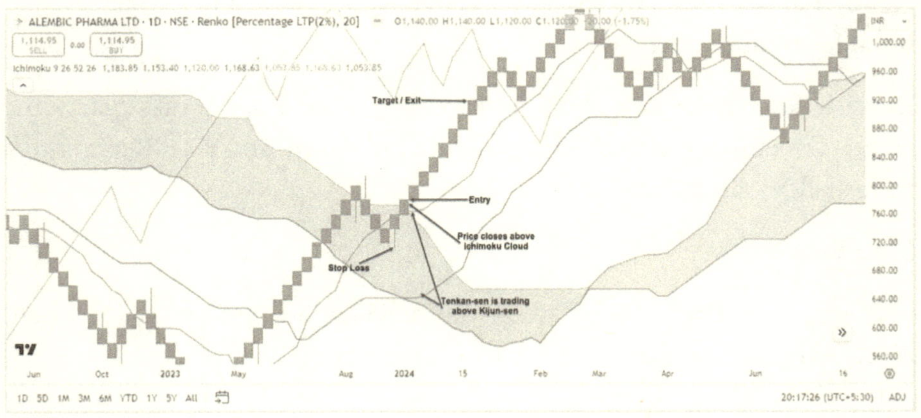

CCI Cycles

The Commodity Channel Index (CCI) is a lesser-known but highly effective indicator. In this chapter, you'll explore strategies like CCI Cyclical Momentum, which identifies cyclical trends within markets. The CCI/Candlestick Reversal strategy merges CCI with candlestick patterns to confirm reversals. Use the CCI Divergence Momentum strategy to detect hidden opportunities where price action and CCI diverge. The CCI Squeeze & Breakout focuses on periods of low volatility followed by explosive moves, while CCI Renko Reversals combine CCI with Renko charts for clearer trends. Whether you're trading trending or range-bound markets, CCI offers a fresh perspective to refine your entries and exits.

31

CCI Cyclical Momentum Strategy

Commodity Channel Index (CCI) is a momentum - based oscillator that measures the difference between the current Price and its average price over a particular period.

Entry:

Bullish Signal: Enter a long position when the CCI (50) crosses above zero and CCI (14) trades above 100.

Bearish Signal: Enter a short position when the CCI (50) crosses below zero and CCI (14) trades below- 100.

Stop Loss:

The stop loss should be based on the previous Swing Low/Swing High, ATR (Average True Range), or any other indicator.

Exit Rules:

Profit Target: Your profit target should be based on your risk - reward ratio. It could be a specific percentage gain or a resistance/support level.

Trailing Stop: You can trail stop - loss to maximize your profit and ride the total momentum as the price moves in your favor.

Risk Management:

Position Sizing: Determine the appropriate size based on your risk tolerance and account size. You should park only 5% of your Capital at a time.

Risk - Reward Ratio: Ensure that your potential profit is significantly greater than your potential loss for each trade. It would help if you kept your Risk - Reward ratio at least 1:2.

Example:

For a Bullish example, refer to the attached chart of Apollo Hospitals. On Jun 11, 2024, CCI (50) crosses above zero, and CCI (14) trades at 207.34, i.e. above 100. We take entry (buy stock) at 6150.00 with a stop loss of 5700.00 (Previous Swing low/Support) and Target of 7050.00 (1:2). The Risk: reward achieved is 1:2, and the Target hit on Sep 12, 2024, with 14.63% profit on deployed Capital.

32

CCI/Candlestick Reversal Strategy

The Commodity Channel Index (CCI) measures the deviation of the Price from its statistical mean. CCI oscillates above and below a zero line. Readings above +100 indicate overbought conditions, while readings below- 100 indicate oversold conditions. Familiarize yourself with patterns like Doji, Hammer, Shooting Star, Engulfing patterns, Morubozu, etc. These patterns can signal potential trend reversals.

Entry:

Bullish Signal: Enter a long position when the CCI rises from oversold levels, forming a bullish candlestick pattern.

Bearish Signal: Enter a short position when the CCI turns down from overbought levels and a bearish candlestick pattern forms.

Stop Loss:

The stop loss should be based on the previous Swing Low/Swing High, ATR (Average True Range), or any other indicator.

Exit Rules:

Profit Target: Your profit target should be based on your risk - reward ratio. It could be a specific percentage gain or a resistance/support level.

Trailing Stop: You can trail stop - loss to maximize your profit and ride the total momentum as the price moves in your favor.

Risk Management:

Position Sizing: Determine the appropriate size based on your risk tolerance and account size. You should park only 5% of your Capital at a time.

Risk - Reward Ratio: Ensure that your potential profit is significantly greater than your potential loss for each trade. It would help if you kept your Risk - Reward ratio at least 1:2.

Example:

For a Bullish example, refer to the attached APTUS Value Housing Finance chart. On Dec 08, 2023, CCI (20) crossed above +100, forming a bullish candle with a big body (almost a Morubozu candle). We take entry (buy stock) at 320.00 with a stop loss of 295.00 (Previous Swing low/Support) and a Target of 370.00 (1:2). The Risk: reward achieved is 1:2, and the Target was hit on Jan 19, 2024, with 15.63% profit on deployed Capital.

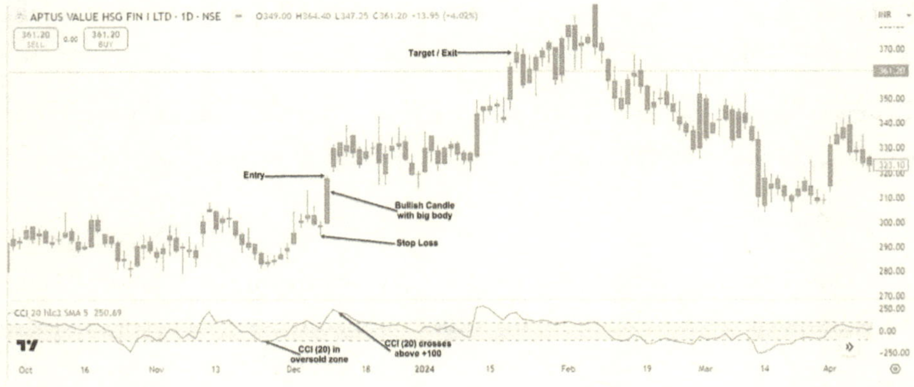

33

CCI Divergence Momentum Strategy

The Commodity Channel Index (CCI) Divergence Momentum strategy is a technical analysis technique to identify potential market trend reversals. This strategy combines the CCI indicator with price action to spot divergences, which can signal upcoming changes in market direction.

Divergence: Bullish Divergence occurs when the Price makes a lower low, but the CCI makes a higher low. Bearish Divergence occurs when the Price makes a higher high, but the CCI makes a lower high.

Entry:

Bullish Signal: Enter a long position when the CCI crosses above the zero line after a bullish diversion, i.e., when Price makes a lower low but the CCI makes a higher low.

Bearish Signal: Enter a short position when the CCI crosses below the zero line after a bearish diversion, i.e., when Price makes a higher high but the CCI makes a lower high.

Stop Loss:

The stop loss should be based on the previous Swing Low/Swing High, ATR (Average True Range), or any other indicator.

Exit Rules:

Profit Target: Your profit target should be based on your risk - reward ratio. It could be a specific percentage gain or a resistance/support level.

Trailing Stop: You can trail stop - loss to maximize your profit and ride the total momentum as the price moves in your favor.

Risk Management:

Position Sizing: Determine the appropriate size based on your risk tolerance and account size. You should park only 5% of your Capital at a time.

Risk - Reward Ratio: Ensure that your potential profit is significantly greater than your potential loss for each trade. It would help if you kept your Risk - Reward ratio at least 1:2.

Example:

For a Bullish example, refer to the attached chart of ASAHI (I) Glass Ltd. Bullish Divergence happened in 2024 on July 3rd and & Aug 1st week. The Price made a lower low, but CCI made a higher low. On Aug 21, 2024, CCI (20) crosses above zero. We take entry (buy stock) at 658.00 with a stop loss of 605.00 (Previous Swing low/Support) and a Target of 765.00 (1:2). The Risk: Reward achieved is 1:2 and Target hit on Sep 20, 2024, with 16.26% profit on deployed Capital.

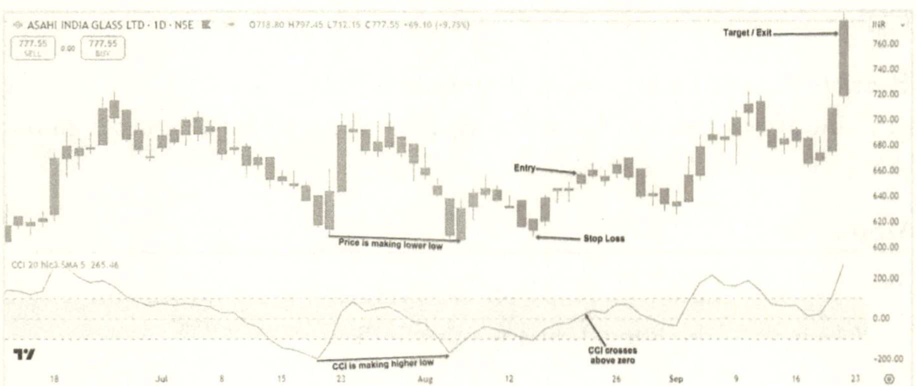

34

CCI Squeeze & Breakout Strategy

The Commodity Channel Index (CCI) Squeeze & Breakout strategy is a famous method traders use to identify potential breakout opportunities. Commodity Channel Index (CCI): Measures the current price level relative to an average price level over a given period. Bollinger Bands: Consists of a middle band (20 - period SMA) and two outer bands (2 standard deviations from the middle band). Keltner Channels: Similar to Bollinger Bands, but uses Average True Range (ATR) for the outer bands instead of standard deviation. Look for periods where the Bollinger Bands are inside the Keltner Channels. This indicates low volatility and is called a "squeeze." Monitor the CCI indicator during the squeeze. Look for the CCI to move above +100 (for a bullish breakout) or below- 100 (for a bearish breakout).

Entry:

Bullish Signal: Enter a long position when the CCI crosses above +100 and the price breaks above the upper Bollinger Band.

Bearish Signal: Enter a short position when the CCI crosses below- 100 and the price breaks below the lower Bollinger Band.

Stop Loss:

The stop loss should be based on the previous Swing Low/Swing High, ATR (Average True Range), or any other indicator.

Exit Rules:

Profit Target: Your profit target should be based on your risk - reward ratio. It could be a specific percentage gain or a resistance or support level.

Trailing Stop: You can trail stop - loss to maximize your profit and ride the total momentum as the price moves in your favor.

Risk Management:

Position Sizing: Determine the appropriate size based on your risk tolerance and account size. You should park only 5% of your Capital at a time.

Risk - Reward Ratio: Ensure that your potential profit is significantly greater than your potential loss for each trade. It would help if you kept your Risk - Reward ratio at least 1:2.

Example:

For a Bullish example, refer to the attached chart of ASTRAZENCA PHARMA. The Bollinger band was trading between Keltner Channel in October 2024. On Nov 09, 2023, the Price crossed above the upper Bollinger Band, and CCI (20) traded above +100. We took entry (buy stock) at 4915.00 with a stop loss of 4475.00 (Previous Swing low/Support) and a Target of 5800.00 (1:2). The Risk: reward achieved is 1:2, and the Target was hit on Jan 10, 2024, with 18.01% profit on deployed Capital.

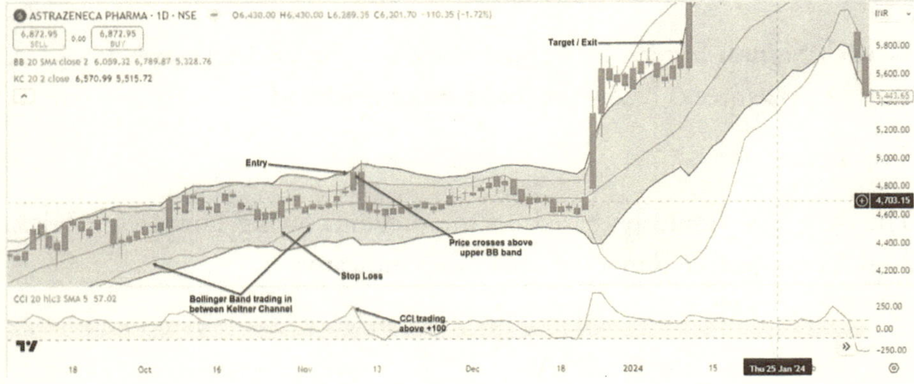

35

CCI Renko Reversals Strategy

CCI is a momentum oscillator that measures the current price level relative to an average price level over a given period. Renko charts use fixed - size blocks (or "bricks") to represent price movements, filtering out minor price movements. In this strategy, we use a Renko chart with a brick size of 2% and a CCI of 14 periods.

Entry:

Bullish Signal: Enter a long position when the Renko chart shows a downtrend (red bricks) and the CCI moves from below- 100 to above zero.

Bearish Signal: Enter a short position when the Renko chart shows an uptrend (green bricks) and the CCI moves from above +100 to below zero.

Stop Loss:

The stop loss should be based on the previous Swing Low/Swing High, ATR (Average True Range), or any other indicator.

Exit Rules:

Profit Target: Your profit target should be based on your risk - reward ratio. It could be a specific percentage gain or a resistance/support level.

Trailing Stop: You can trail stop - loss to maximize your profit and ride the total momentum as the price moves in your favor.

Risk Management:

Position Sizing: Determine the appropriate size based on your risk tolerance and account size. You should park only 5% of your Capital at a time.

Risk - Reward Ratio: Ensure that your potential profit is significantly greater than your potential loss for each trade. It would help if you kept your Risk - Reward ratio at least 1:2.

Example:

For a Bullish example, refer to the attached chart of ADANI Total Gas Ltd. Renko has been making red bricks since May 26, 2023, and CCI also crossed below- 100. On Nov 28, 2023, Renko started making green bricks, and CCI crossed above- 100; on the same day, CCI crossed above zero. We take entry (buy stock) at 615.00 with a stop loss of 530.00 (Previous Swing low/Support) and Target of 790.00 (1:2). The Risk: Reward achieved is 1:2 and Target hit on Dec 05 2023 with 28.46% profit on deployed Capital.

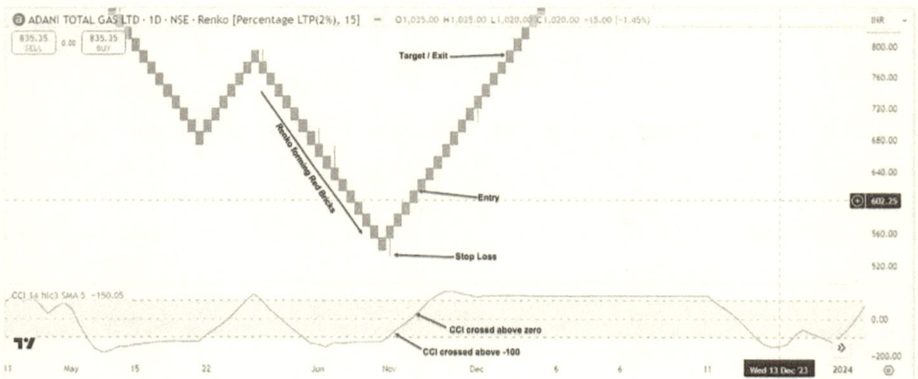

Awesome Oscillators

The Awesome Oscillator (AO) is simple yet effective for identifying market momentum. This chapter covers six strategies. The Awesome Oscillator Saucer Trades focus on identifying bullish and bearish reversals using the saucer pattern. Use AO/MACD Two-Timeframe strategies to align trends across multiple timeframes. The AO & MA Zone Cross strategy integrates moving averages for dynamic confirmation. For momentum traders, the AO & RSI Power strategy combines two oscillators for strong signals. Learn to spot breakout opportunities with AO Squeeze & Breakout, and use AO Heikin-Ashi Smoothing to filter market noise. You'll discover how AO can confirm trends and alert you to potential reversals, giving you an edge in volatile markets.

36

Awesome Oscillators
Saucer Trades Strategy

The Awesome Oscillator is a momentum indicator that shows the difference between a 34 - period and 5 - period simple moving average of the candlestick midpoints ((H+L)/2).

Bullish Saucer forms when the AO is above the zero line. There are three consecutive bars on the AO: the first bar is red, the Second bar is red but higher than the first (less negative), and the Third bar is green.

Bearish Saucer forms when the AO is below the zero line. The AO has three consecutive bars: the first bar is green, the Second bar is green but lower than the first (less positive), and the Third bar is red.

Entry:

Bullish Signal: Enter a long position when the bullish saucer pattern's third (green) bar forms.

Bearish Signal: Enter a short position when the bearish saucer pattern's third (red) bar forms.

Stop Loss:

The stop loss should be based on the previous Swing Low/Swing High, ATR (Average True Range), or any other indicator.

Exit Rules:

Profit Target: Your profit target should be based on your risk - reward ratio. It could be a specific percentage gain or a resistance/support level.

Trailing Stop: You can trail stop - loss to maximize your profit and ride the total momentum as the price moves in your favor.

Risk Management:

Position Sizing: Determine the appropriate size based on your risk tolerance and account size. You should park only 5% of your Capital at a time.

Risk - Reward Ratio: Ensure that your potential profit is significantly greater than your potential loss for each trade. It would help if you kept your Risk - Reward ratio at least 1:2.

Example:

For a Bullish example, refer to the attached chart of ATUL Ltd. Bullish saucer patterns formed between Jun 27, 2024, and Jul 01, 2024. We took entry (buy stock) at 6590.00 with a stop loss of 6280.00 (Previous Swing low/Support) and a Target of 7210.00 (1:2). The Risk: reward achieved is 1:2, and the Target was hit on Jul 22, 2024, with a 9.41% profit on deployed Capital.

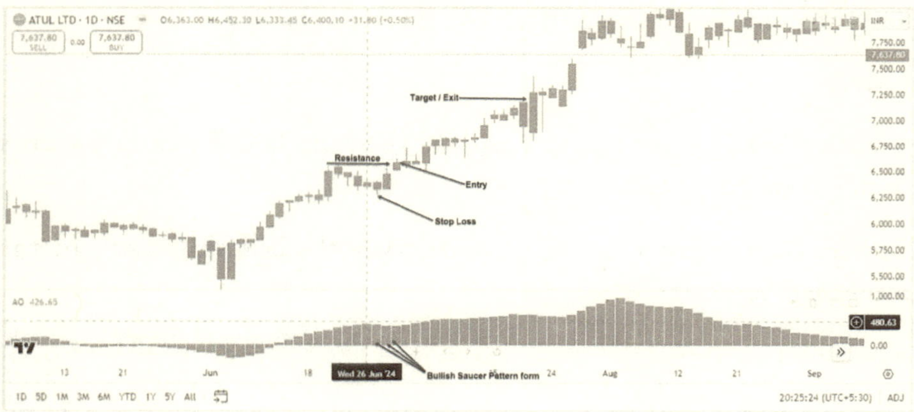

37

AO/MACD Two – Time Frame Strategy

The Awesome Oscillator (AO) and Moving Average Convergence Divergence (MACD) are technical indicators that you can use together to provide more reliable signals for trend direction and market momentum. MACD: Helps identify entry and exit price levels. It reacts faster than the AO and provides earlier signals. AO confirms the price levels determined by the MACD.

The strategy is based on the idea that the MACD produces a signal in a lower time frame (60 min in our case), and the AO confirms it in a higher time frame (Daily in our case). A bullish MACD crossover can be confirmed by the AO entering the positive zone.

Entry:

Bullish Signal: Enter a long position when the higher time frame AO shows a bullish trend (green bar above zero line) and the lower time frame MACD line crosses above the signal line. To double sure, we can wait for a price breakout.

Bearish Signal: Enter a short position when the higher time frame AO shows a bearish trend (red bar below zero line) and the lower time frame MACD line crosses below the signal line. To double sure, we can wait for the price breakdown.

Stop Loss:

The stop loss should be based on the previous Swing Low/Swing High, ATR (Average True Range), or any other indicator.

Exit Rules:

Profit Target: Your profit target should be based on your risk - reward ratio. It could be a specific percentage gain or a resistance/support level.

Trailing Stop: You can trail stop - loss to maximize your profit and ride the total momentum as the price moves in your favor.

Risk Management:

Position Sizing: Determine the appropriate size based on your risk tolerance and account size. You should park only 5% of your Capital at a time.

Risk - Reward Ratio: Ensure that your potential profit is significantly greater than your potential loss for each trade. It would help if you kept your Risk - Reward ratio at least 1:2.

Example:

For a Bullish example, refer to the attached chart of Bajaj Holdings. On Jun 24, 2024, the MACD (LTF) line crosses above zero & the signal line, the AO (HTF), forms a green candle above zero, and the Price breaks out of the previous swing high. We take entry (buy stock) at 8725.00 with a stop loss of 7655.00 (Previous Swing low/Support) and Target of 10900.00 (1:2). The Risk: Reward achieved is 1:2 and Target hit on Sep 03 2024 with 24.93% profit on deployed Capital.

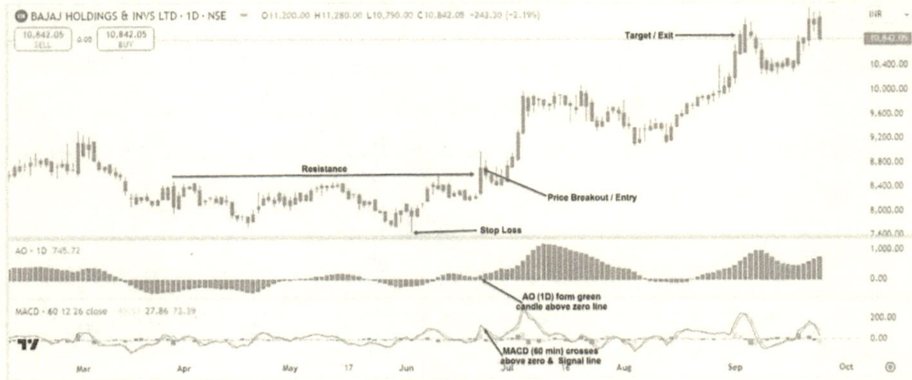

38

AO MA Zone Cross Strategy

The area between the fast and slow Moving Averages is the MA Zone. When Price is above both MAs, it's bullish. When the Price is below both MAs, it's bearish. When Price is between the MAs, it's in a neutral zone. AO crossing above the zero line with Green bars indicates bullish momentum, and below the zero line with Red bars indicates bearish momentum.

In this strategy, we look for the script to trade above/below both MAs and the AO to trade above/below the zero line.

Entry:

Bullish Signal: Enter a long position when the Price crosses above the MA Zone (moves above both 20 & 50 MAs) and AO is above the zero line or crossing above it. To double sure, we can wait for a price breakout.

Bearish Signal: Enter a short position when the Price crosses below the MA Zone (moves below both 20 & 50 MAs) and AO is below the zero line or crossing below it. To double sure, we can wait for the price breakdown.

Stop Loss:

The stop loss should be based on the previous Swing Low/Swing High, ATR (Average True Range), or any other indicator.

Exit Rules:

Profit Target: Your profit target should be based on your risk - reward ratio. It could be a specific percentage gain or a resistance/support level.

Trailing Stop: You can trail stop - loss to maximize your profit and ride the total momentum as the price moves in your favor.

Risk Management:

Position Sizing: Determine the appropriate size based on your risk tolerance and account size. You should park only 5% of your Capital at a time.

Risk - Reward Ratio: Ensure that your potential profit is significantly greater than your potential loss for each trade. It would help if you kept your Risk - Reward ratio at least 1:2.

Example:

For a Bullish example, refer to the attached chart of Bajaj Auto Ltd. On Aug 07, 2024, the Price closes above MAs 20 & 50, and AO crosses above zero with green candle formation, but we await price action. On Aug 23, 2024, the price was still trading above both MAs, i.e., 20 & 50, and AO was trading above zero with green candle formation. Also, the Price breaks out of the previous swing high. We take entry (buy stock) at 10405.00 with a stop loss of 9370.00 (Previous Swing low/Support) and Target of 12475.00 (1:2). The Risk: Reward achieved is 1:2 and Target hit on Sep 24, 2024, with 19.89% profit on deployed Capital.

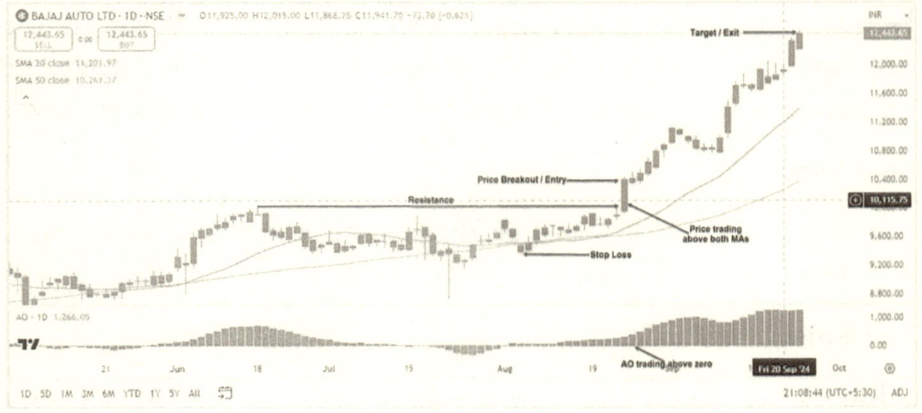

39

AO & RSI Power Strategy

The AO & RSI strategy combines two powerful technical indicators to identify potential trading opportunities. The Awesome Oscillator (AO) helps to identify market momentum and possible trend reversals. At the same time, the Relative Strength Index (RSI) measures the speed and change of price movements, indicating overbought or oversold conditions. We can make more informed decisions about market entries and exits using these indicators.

Entry:

Bullish Signal: Enter a long position when the AO crosses above the zero line or shows increasing green bars and RSI moves above 30 from oversold territory. To double sure, we can wait for a price breakout.

Bearish Signal: Enter a short position when the AO crosses below the zero line or shows increasing red bars and RSI moves below 70 from overbought territory. To double sure, we can wait for the price breakdown.

Stop Loss:

The stop loss should be based on the previous Swing Low/Swing High, ATR (Average True Range), or any other indicator.

Exit Rules:

Profit Target: Your profit target should be based on your risk - reward ratio. It could be a specific percentage gain or a resistance/support level.

Trailing Stop: You can trail stop - loss to maximize your profit and ride the total momentum as the price moves in your favor.

Risk Management:

Position Sizing: Determine the appropriate size based on your risk tolerance and account size. You should park only 5% of your Capital at a time.

Risk - Reward Ratio: Ensure that your potential profit is significantly greater than your potential loss for each trade. It would help if you kept your Risk - Reward ratio at least 1:2.

Example:

For a Bullish example, refer to the attached chart of Bajaj Finance Ltd. On Apr 18, 2023, AO crossed above zero with green candle formation, and RSI was trading above 30, but we waited for price action. On Apr 25, 2023, AO is still trading above zero with green candle formation and RSI trading above 30. Also, the Price breaks out of the previous swing high. We take entry (buy stock) at 6075.00 with a stop loss of 5530.00 (Previous Swing low/Support) and Target of 7170.00 (1:2). The Risk: Reward achieved is 1:2 and Target hit on Jun 13, 2023, with 18.02% profit on deployed Capital.

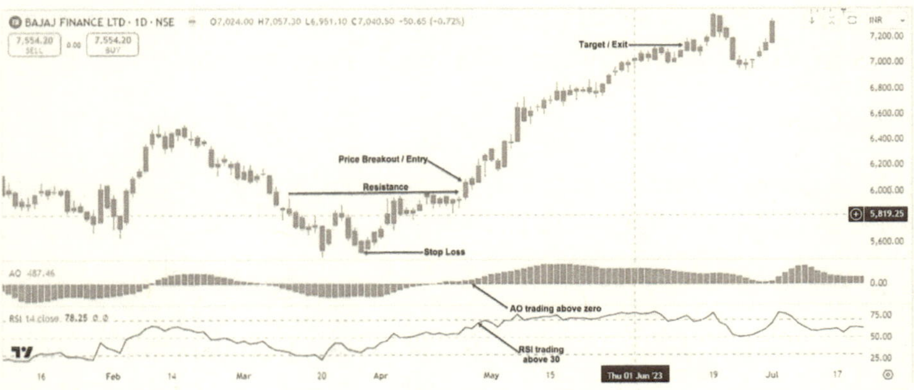

40

AO Squeeze & Breakout Strategy

The AO Squeeze & Breakout strategy combines the Awesome Oscillator (AO) indicator with a volatility squeeze to identify potential breakout opportunities. This method is beneficial for traders looking to capitalize on momentum after periods of consolidation.

In this strategy, we will look for a period when Bollinger Bands narrow and converge with Keltner Channels. This indicates decreasing volatility and potential energy building up for a breakout. Watch for the AO to cross above or below the zero line. A bullish signal occurs when the AO crosses above zero; bearish when it crosses below zero.

Entry:

Bullish Signal: Enter a long position when the AO crosses/trades above the zero line and Price closes above the upper Bollinger Band.

Bearish Signal: Enter a short position when the AO crosses/trades below the zero line and Price closes below the lower Bollinger Band.

Stop Loss:

The stop loss should be based on the previous Swing Low/Swing High, ATR (Average True Range), or any other indicator.

Exit Rules:

Profit Target: Your profit target should be based on your risk - reward ratio. It could be a specific percentage gain or a resistance/support level.

Trailing Stop: You can trail stop - loss to maximize your profit and ride the total momentum as the price moves in your favor.

Risk Management:

Position Sizing: Determine the appropriate size based on your risk tolerance and account size. You should park only 5% of your Capital at a time.

Risk - Reward Ratio: Ensure that your potential profit is significantly greater than your potential loss for each trade. It would help if you kept your Risk - Reward ratio at least 1:2.

Example:

For a Bullish example, refer to the attached chart of Balkrishna Industries Ltd. On Mar 28, 2024, AO crosses above zero in squeezed BB & KC with green candle formation. On Apr 05, 2024, AO was still trading above zero with green candle formation, and Price crossed above the upper band of BB. We take entry (buy stock) at 2405.00 with a stop loss of 2190.00 (Previous Swing low/Support) and Target of 2840.00 (1:2). The Risk: Reward achieved is 1:2.29 and Target hit on May 21 2024 (2898.00) with 20.50% profit on deployed Capital.

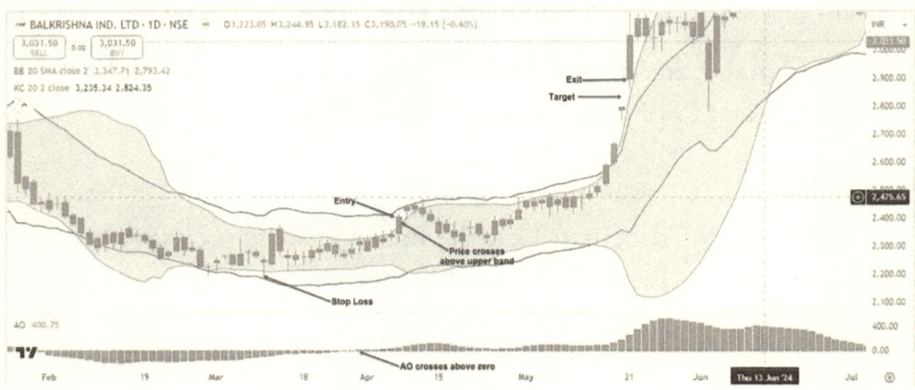

41

AO Heikin – Ashi Smoothing Strategy

The AO Heikin - Ashi Smoothing strategy combines the Awesome Oscillator (AO) with Heikin - Ashi candlesticks to identify trends and potential reversals. This method aims to smooth out price action and provide more precise signals for entry and exit points. It is beneficial for beginners looking to reduce noise in their trading decisions.

Entry:

Bullish Signal: Enter a long position when the AO crosses/trades above the zero line. Heikin Ashi candles are predominantly green with little or no lower shadows.

Bearish Signal: Enter a short position when the AO crosses/trades below the zero line. Heikin Ashi candles are predominantly red with little or no upper shadows.

Stop Loss:

The stop loss should be the previous Swing Low/Swing High, ATR (Average True Range), or any other indicator.

Exit Rules:

Profit Target: Your profit target should be based on your risk - reward ratio. It could be a specific percentage gain or a resistance/support level.

Trailing Stop: You can trail stop - loss to maximize your profit and ride the full momentum as the price moves in your favor.

Risk Management:

Position Sizing: Determine the appropriate size based on your risk tolerance and account size. You should park only 5% of your Capital at a time.

Risk - Reward Ratio: Ensure that your potential profit is significantly greater than your potential loss for each trade. It would help if you kept your Risk - Reward ratio at least 1:2.

Example:

Refer to the attached Balrampur Chini Mills Ltd chart for a Bullish example. On 07th June 2024, AO crossed above zero with a green candle formation, and the Heikin Ashi candle is also green with no lower wick. We took entry (buy stock) at 396.00 with a stop loss of 350.00 (Previous Swing low/Support) and a Target of 488.00 (1:2). The Risk: reward achieved is 1:2, and the Target hit on 31st July 2024 with 23.23% profit on deployed capital.

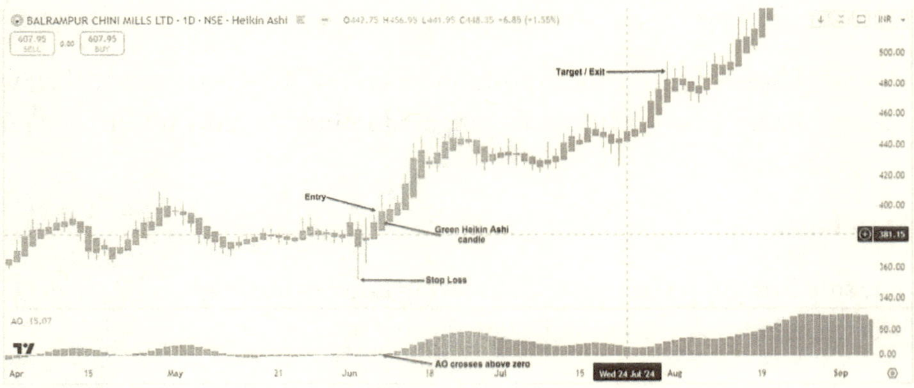

Bollinger Bands

Bollinger Bands are the go-to tool for volatility-based trading. This chapter provides six beginner-friendly strategies. The Standard Bollinger Bands strategy teaches you to trade price reversals at the upper and lower bands. The Bollinger Squeeze & Expansion identifies periods of low volatility that precede big moves. Combine Bollinger Candlestick Patterns for precise entries and exits. For a multi-indicator approach, try Bollinger, MACD & RSI Confluence or Bollinger & OBV setups. Finally, the Bollinger & Keltner Channels strategy highlights explosive breakouts when these bands align. Learn how to use Bollinger Bands to predict price breakouts and identify optimal trade setups, even in unpredictable markets.

42

Standard Bollinger Bands Strategy

Bollinger Bands measures market volatility and identifies potential overbought or oversold conditions. They consist of three lines: a middle band (typically a 20 - day simple moving average) and upper and lower bands, two standard deviations from the middle band.

Entry:

Bullish Signal: Enter a long position when the price touches or falls below the lower Bollinger Band, indicating potentially oversold conditions and a bounce back to the middle or upper band.

Bearish Signal: Enter a short position when the price touches or rises above the upper Bollinger Band, signaling potential overbought conditions and a retracement back to the middle or lower band.

Stop Loss:

The stop loss should be a lower band or candle low in case of buying and an upper band or candle high in case of shorting.

Exit Rules:

Profit Target: The profit target should be the upper band when buying and the lower band when shorting.

Trailing Stop: You can trail your stop - loss until the candle closes below the midline of BB to maximize your profit and ride the full momentum as the price moves in your favor.

Risk Management:

Position Sizing: Determine the appropriate size based on your risk tolerance and account size. You should park only 5% of your Capital at a time.

Risk - Reward Ratio: Ensure that your potential profit is significantly greater than your potential loss for each trade. It would help if you kept your Risk - Reward ratio at least 1:2.

Example:

For a bullish example, refer to the attached chart for BANDHAN BANK. On 28th March 23, the Price touched the lower band and started reversing. On 06th April 2023, the Price closed above mid - band. We took entry (buy stock) at 208.00 with a stop loss of 182.00 (Previous Swing low/Support) and a Target of 260.00 (1:2). The Risk: reward achieved is 1:2, and the Target hit on 24th May 2023 with a 25.00% profit on deployed capital.

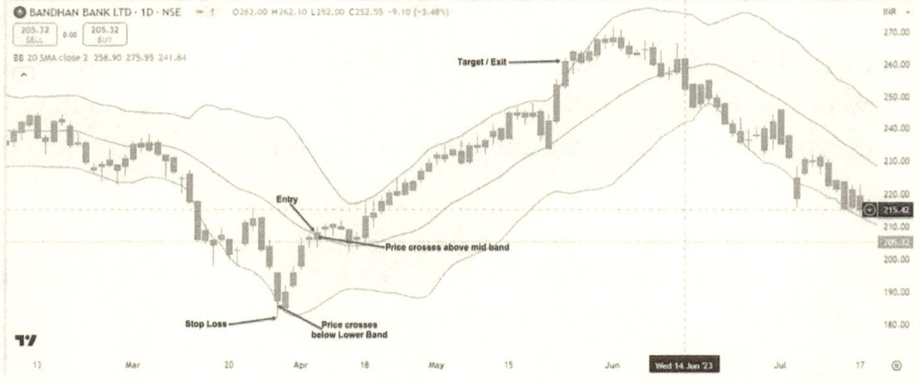

43

Bollinger Squeeze & Expansion Strategy

Bollinger Band Squeeze strategy is used to identify periods of low volatility characterized by narrow price ranges or consolidations.

Entry:

Bullish Signal: Enter a long position when the Price breaks out above the upper boundary of the Bollinger Band, indicating a potential bullish breakout.

Bearish Signal: Enter a short position when the Price breaks down below the lower boundary of the Bollinger Band, signaling a potential bearish breakout.

Stop Loss:

Stop loss should be previous Swing low/high, Support/Resistance, or any other indicator.

Exit Rules:

Profit Target: Your profit target should be based on your risk - reward ratio. It could be a specific percentage gain or the next Support/Resistance.

Trailing Stop: You can trail stop - loss to maximize your profit and ride the full momentum as the price moves in your favor.

Risk Management:

Position Sizing: Determine the appropriate size based on your risk tolerance and account size. You should park only 5% of your Capital at a time.

Risk - Reward Ratio: Ensure that your potential profit is significantly greater than your potential loss for each trade. It would help if you kept your Risk - Reward ratio at least 1:2.

Example:

For a Bullish example, refer to the attached chart of Deepak Nitrite. On 13th Apr - 23, the Price crossed above the squeezed Bollinger Band upper line and broke the previous swing high. We took entry (buy stock) at 1875.00 with a stop loss at 1760.00 (Previous Swing Low) and a Target of 2105.00 (R: R 1:2). The Risk: reward achieved is 1:2, and the Target hit on 24[th]May - 23 with a 12.27% profit on deployed capital.

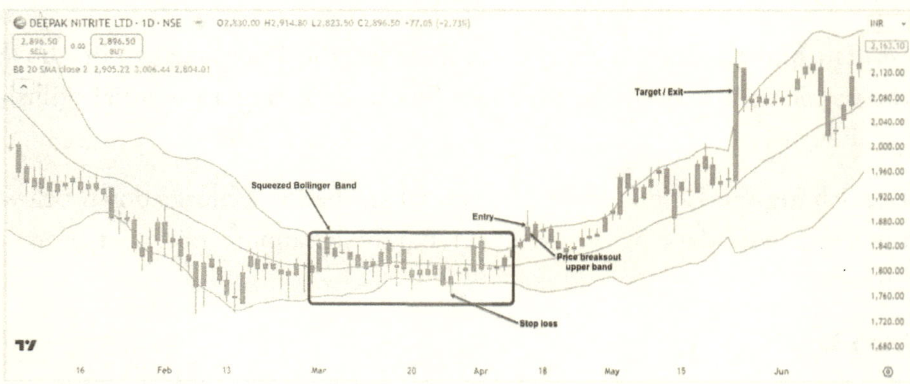

44

Bollinger Candlestick Patterns Strategy

Bollinger Candlestick Patterns combine two powerful technical analysis tools: Bollinger Bands and candlestick patterns. This approach helps traders accurately identify potential trend reversals, continuations, and breakouts. Watch for candlesticks touching or breaking through the bands.

Entry:

Bullish Signal: Enter a long position when the bullish candlestick patterns form near the bands.

Bearish Signal: Enter a short position when the bearish candlestick patterns form near the bands.

Stop Loss:

Stop loss should be previous Swing low/high, Support/Resistance, or any other indicator.

Exit Rules:

Profit Target: Your profit target should be based on your risk - reward ratio. It could be a specific percentage gain or the next Support/Resistance.

Trailing Stop: You can trail stop - loss to maximize your profit and ride the full momentum as the price moves in your favor.

Risk Management:

Position Sizing: Determine the appropriate size based on your risk tolerance and account size. You should park only 5% of your Capital at a time.

Risk - Reward Ratio: Ensure that your potential profit is significantly greater than your potential loss for each trade. It would help if you kept your Risk - Reward ratio at least 1:2.

Example:

For a Bullish example, refer to the attached chart of BANK OF BARODA. On 27[th]October 2023, a bullish piercing candle formed after the previous candle closed below the lower band of Bollinger, indicating a reversal. We take entry (buy stock) at 197.00 with a stop loss at 187.00 (Previous Swing Low) and a Target of 217.00 (R: R 1:2). The Risk: reward achieved is 1:2, and the Target hit on 13[th]Dec - 23 with 10.15% profit on deployed capital.

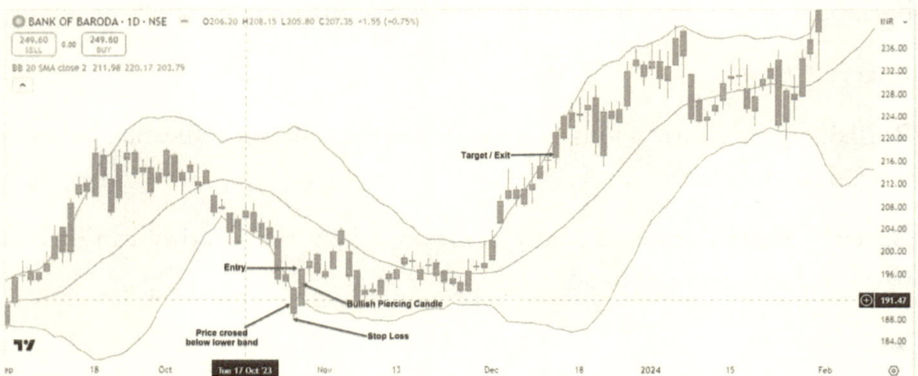

45

Bollinger, MACD & RSI Confluence Strategy

The Bollinger Bands, MACD (Moving Average Convergence Divergence), and RSI (Relative Strength Index) confluence strategy combines three technical indicators to identify high - probability trading opportunities. This strategy helps confirm trends, spot potential reversals, and filter out false signals.

Entry:

Bullish Signal: Enter a long position when the Price crosses above the middle band of Bollinger and bands expand, the MACD line crosses above the signal line, and the RSI crosses above 70.

Bearish Signal: Enter a short position when the Price crosses below the middle band of Bollinger and bands expand, the MACD line crosses below the signal line, and the RSI crosses below 30.

Stop Loss:

Stop loss should be previous Swing low/high, Support/Resistance, or any other indicator.

Exit Rules:

Profit Target: Your profit target should be based on your risk - reward ratio. It could be a specific percentage gain or the next Support/Resistance.

Trailing Stop: You can trail stop - loss to maximize your profit and ride the full momentum as the price moves in your favor.

Risk Management:

Position Sizing: Determine the appropriate size based on your risk tolerance and account size. You should park only 5% of your Capital at a time.

Risk - Reward Ratio: Ensure that your potential profit is significantly greater than your potential loss for each trade. It would help if you kept your Risk - Reward ratio at least 1:2.

Example:

For a Bullish example, refer to the attached chart of BOMBAY BURMAH. On 24[th]Jun - 2024, the Price was trading above the middle band of Bollinger, and the band was expanding. The MACD line was above the signal line, and the RSI crossed above 70. We took entry (buy stock) at 2015.00 with a stop loss at 1600.00 (Previous Swing Low) and a Target of 2850.00 (R: R 1:2). The Risk: reward achieved is 1:2, and the Target hit on 27[th]Sep - 2024 with 41.44% profit on deployed capital.

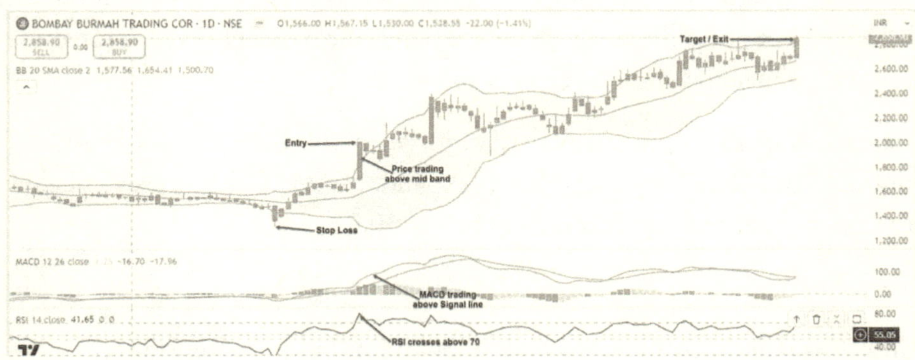

46

Bollinger & OBV Strategy

Bollinger Bands and OBV technical tools identify potential entry and exit points in the stock market. When combined, these indicators can provide valuable insights into price trends and volume patterns.

Entry:

Bullish Signal: Enter a long position when, after touching/crossing below the lower band, Price crosses above the mid/high band of Bollinger, and OBV shows an upward trend.

Bearish Signal: Enter a short position after touching/crossing above the upper band. The price crossed below Bollinger's mid/low band, and OBV shows a downward trend.

Stop Loss:

Stop loss should be previous Swing low/high, Support/Resistance, or any other indicator.

Exit Rules:

Profit Target: Your profit target should be based on your risk - reward ratio. It could be a specific percentage gain or the next Support/Resistance.

Trailing Stop: You can trail stop - loss to maximize your profit and ride the full momentum as the price moves in your favor.

Risk Management:

Position Sizing: Determine the appropriate size based on your risk tolerance and account size. You should park only 5% of your Capital at a time.

Risk - Reward Ratio: Ensure that your potential profit is significantly greater than your potential loss for each trade. It would help if you kept your Risk - Reward ratio at least 1:2.

Example:

For a Bullish example, refer to the attached chart of BHARAT DYNAMICS LTD. After breaching the lower band on 13th March 2024, prices increased. On 23rd April 2024, the Price crossed above the higher band of Bollinger, and the OBV rose. We take entry (buy stock) at 962.00 with a stop loss at 840.00 (Previous Swing Low) and a Target of 1206.00 (R: R 1:2). The Risk: reward achieved is 1:2, and the Target hit on 18thMay 2024 with 25.36% profit on deployed capital.

47

Bollinger & Keltner Channels Strategy

Bollinger Bands and Keltner Channels are popular volatility indicators used in technical analysis. They can provide powerful insights into market volatility, potential breakouts, and trend strength. This strategy is beneficial for identifying squeeze conditions and potential high - probability trading opportunities.

A squeeze occurs when Bollinger Bands are inside Keltner Channels. This indicates low volatility and the potential for a breakout. Watch for the squeeze release: When Bollinger Bands move outside Keltner Channels, it signals increasing volatility. Determine the trend direction: Uptrend - Price breaks above both the upper Bollinger Band and Keltner Channel; Downtrend - Price breaks below both the lower Bollinger Band and Keltner Channel.

Entry:

Bullish Signal: Enter a long position when Price breaks above both upper bands (Bollinger and Keltner Channel) during a squeeze release.

Bearish Signal: Enter a short position when Price breaks below both lower bands (Bollinger and Keltner Channel) during a squeeze release.

Stop Loss:

Stop loss should be previous Swing low/high, Support/Resistance, or any other indicator.

Exit Rules:

Profit Target: Your profit target should be based on your risk - reward ratio. It could be a specific percentage gain or the next Support/Resistance.

Trailing Stop: You can trail stop - loss to maximize your profit and ride the full momentum as the price moves in your favor.

Risk Management:

Position Sizing: Determine the appropriate size based on your risk tolerance and account size. You should park only 5% of your Capital at a time.

Risk - Reward Ratio: Ensure that your potential profit is significantly greater than your potential loss for each trade. It would help if you kept your Risk - Reward ratio at least 1:2.

Example:

For a Bullish example, refer to the attached chart of BHARAT ELECTRONICS LTD. A squeeze occurs between 18th January and 22nd February 2024. On 23rd February 24, the price broke out in both higher bands. We took an entry (buy stock) at 205.00 with a stop loss at 171.00 (the Previous Swing Low) and a Target of 273.00 (R: R 1:2). The Risk: reward achieved is 1:2, and the Target hit on 21st May 2024 with a 33.17% profit on deployed capital.

Parabolic Adventures

The Parabolic SAR indicator is designed to pinpoint trend direction and reversals. This chapter covers five strategies. The Parabolic SAR (Stop and Reverse) Strategy teaches you to identify trends with clear stop levels. Use the Parabolic SAR & EMA Pullback strategy to trade pullbacks within a trend. The Parabolic SAR & Stochastics Divergence strategy helps you spot divergence setups for early reversals. Parabolic Squeeze & Breakout focuses on breakout opportunities, while Parabolic SAR & Renko Strategy simplifies trend analysis with Renko charts. Easy to follow, these strategies help beginners identify clear entry and exit points, especially in trending markets.

48

Parabolic SAR (Stop and Reverse) Strategy

Parabolic SAR indicates potential trend reversals and trailing stop - loss levels. This indicator suggests an uptrend if the dots display underneath Price and indicates a downtrend if the dots display above Price. You can use the Parabolic SAR dots as dynamic trailing stop - loss levels to protect profits and manage trade exits as the trend develops.

Entry:

Bullish Signal: Enter a long position when the Parabolic SAR dots move below the Price. This indicates a bullish reversal and potential continuation of the uptrend.

Bearish Signal: Enter a short position when the Parabolic SAR dots move above the Price, signaling a bearish reversal and potential continuation of the downtrend.

Stop Loss:

Stop loss should be based on Parabolic SAR, Support/Resistance, or any other indicator.

Exit Rules:

Profit Target: Your profit target should be based on your risk - reward ratio. It could be a specific percentage gain or the next Support/Resistance.

Trailing Stop: You can trail stop - loss using Parabolic SAR to maximize your profit and ride the full momentum as the price moves in your favor.

Risk Management:

Position Sizing: Determine the appropriate size based on your risk tolerance and account size. You should park only 5% of your Capital at a time.

Risk - Reward Ratio: Ensure that your potential profit is significantly greater than your potential loss for each trade. It would help if you kept your Risk - Reward ratio at least 1:2.

Example:

Refer to the attached APL Apollo Tubes (APLAPOLLO) chart for a Bullish example. After a downtrend on15[th] February 2024, the Parabolic SAR dot displayed below Price (indicating reversal, i.e., an uptrend). We take entry (buy stock) at 1420.00 with a stop loss at 1300.00 (Support at the previous swing low) and a Target of 1660.00 (R: R 1:2). The Risk: reward achieved is 1:2, and the Target hit on 17th May2024 with 16.90% profit on deployed capital.

49

Parabolic SAR & EMA Pullback Strategy

The Parabolic SAR & EMA Pullback strategy combines two popular technical indicators: Parabolic SAR for trend direction and potential reversal points and the Exponential Moving Average (EMA) for identifying pullbacks within the trend. This combination can help traders enter trends with better timing and potentially reduce false signals.

Entry:

Bullish Signal: Enter a long position when Price pulls back to the faster EMA in an uptrend and starts moving up. Ensure the SAR dots are still below Price, i.e., in an uptrend.

Bearish Signal: Enter a short position when Price pulls up to the faster EMA in a downtrend and start's moving down. Ensure the SAR dots are still above Price, i.e., in a downtrend.

Stop Loss:

Stop loss should be based on Parabolic SAR, Support/Resistance, or any other indicator.

Exit Rules:

Profit Target: Your profit target should be based on your risk - reward ratio. It could be a specific percentage gain or the next Support/Resistance.

Trailing Stop: You can trail your stop loss using Parabolic SAR to maximize your profit and ride the full momentum as the price moves in your favor.

Risk Management:

Position Sizing: Determine the appropriate size based on your risk tolerance and account size. You should park only 5% of your Capital at a time.

Risk - Reward Ratio: Ensure that your potential profit is significantly greater than your potential loss for each trade. It would help if you kept your Risk - Reward ratio at least 1:2.

Example:

For a Bullish example, refer to the attached chart of Apollo Tyres Ltd. On 09th November 2023, 20 EMA crossed above 50 EMA in an uptrend (Parabolic SAR is trading below Price). A pullback happens between the 20th & 24th Nov 2023. After the breakout of the pullback swing high, we take entry (buy stock) on 01st December 2023 at 443.00 with a stop loss at 413.00 (Support at previous swing low) and Target of 503.00 (R: R 1:2). The Risk: Reward achieved is 1:2, and Target hit on 18th January 2024 with 13.54% profit on deployed capital.

50

Parabolic SAR & Stochastics Divergence Strategy

Parabolic SAR (Stop and Reverse) and Stochastic Oscillators are technical indicators traders use to identify potential trend reversals and divergences in price action. Combining these two indicators can provide more substantial trade entry and exit point signals.

Entry:

Bullish Signal: Enter a long position when the SAR dots move below Price and there is bullish Stochastic divergence i.e., Price makes lower lows, but Stochastic makes higher lows.

Bearish Signal: Enter a short position when the SAR dots move above Price, and there is bearish Stochastic divergence i.e., Price makes higher highs, but Stochastic makes lower highs.

Stop Loss:

Stop loss should be based on Parabolic SAR, Support/Resistance, or any other indicator.

Exit Rules:

Profit Target: Your profit target should be based on your risk - reward ratio. It could be a specific percentage gain or the next Support/Resistance.

Trailing Stop: You can trail your stop loss using Parabolic SAR to maximize your profit and ride the full momentum as the price moves in your favor.

Risk Management:

Position Sizing: Determine the appropriate size based on your risk tolerance and account size. You should park only 5% of your Capital at a time.

Risk - Reward Ratio: Ensure that your potential profit is significantly greater than your potential loss for each trade. It would help if you kept your Risk - Reward ratio at least 1:2.

Example:

For a Bullish example, refer to the attached chart of Asian Paints Ltd. Between 19th April & 10th May 2024, there is a bullish diversion, i.e., Price makes a lower low whereas Stochastics makes higher lows. On 23rd May 2024, SAR started trading below Price. We take entry (buy stock) at 2905.00 with a stop loss at 2670.00 (Support at previous swing low) and a Target of 3375.00 (R: R 1:2). The Risk: Reward achieved is 1:2, and Target hit on 11th September 2024 with 16.18% profit on deployed capital.

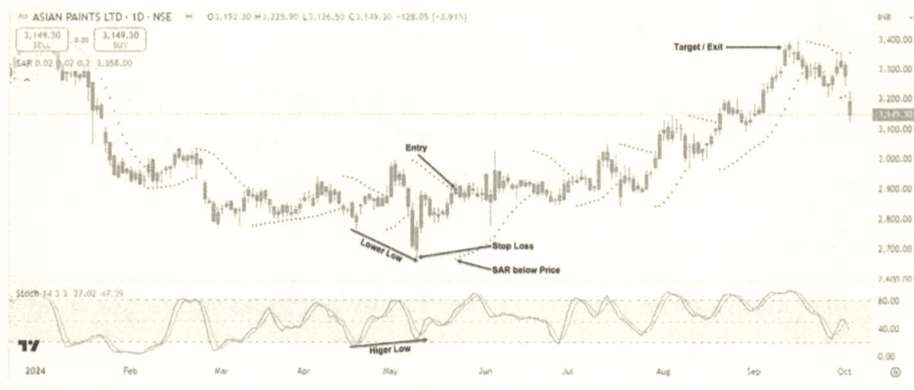

51

Parabolic Squeeze & Breakout Strategy

The Parabolic Squeeze & Breakout strategy combines the Parabolic SAR (Stop and Reverse) indicator with a volatility squeeze concept. This approach aims to identify periods of low volatility (the squeeze) followed by potential breakouts, which can lead to significant price movements.

In this strategy, we look for periods when the Parabolic SAR dots are getting closer to the Price. This compression indicates decreasing volatility (the squeeze). Watch for the Price to start moving more decisively in one direction. This could signal the end of the squeeze and the beginning of a breakout. A breakout occurs when the Price moves significantly away from the Parabolic SAR dots. The dots should flip to the other side of the Price (above for downtrend, below for uptrend).

Entry:

Bullish Signal: Enter a long position when the price breaks above the SAR dots after the squeeze.

Bearish Signal: Enter a short position when the price breaks below the SAR dots after the squeeze.

Stop Loss:

Stop loss should be based on Parabolic SAR, Support/Resistance, or any other indicator.

Exit Rules:

Profit Target: Your profit target should be based on your risk - reward ratio. It could be a specific percentage gain or the next Support/Resistance.

Trailing Stop: You can trail stop - loss using Parabolic SAR to maximize your profit and ride the full momentum as the price moves in your favor.

Risk Management:

Position Sizing: Determine the appropriate size based on your risk tolerance and account size. You should park only 5% of your Capital at a time.

Risk - Reward Ratio: Ensure that your potential profit is significantly greater than your potential loss for each trade. It would help if you kept your Risk - Reward ratio at least 1:2.

Example:

Refer to the attached ASAHI (I) Glass Ltd chart for a Bullish example. In a downtrend, SAR came near Price on 07th June 2024, indicating a squeeze. A breakout happened on 11th June 2024, and SAR started trading below Price. We take entry (buy stock) at 620.00 with a stop loss at 540.00 (Support at previous swing low) and a Target of 780.00 (R: R 1:2). The Risk: Reward achieved is 1:2 and Target hit on 20th September 2024 with 25.81% profit on deployed capital.

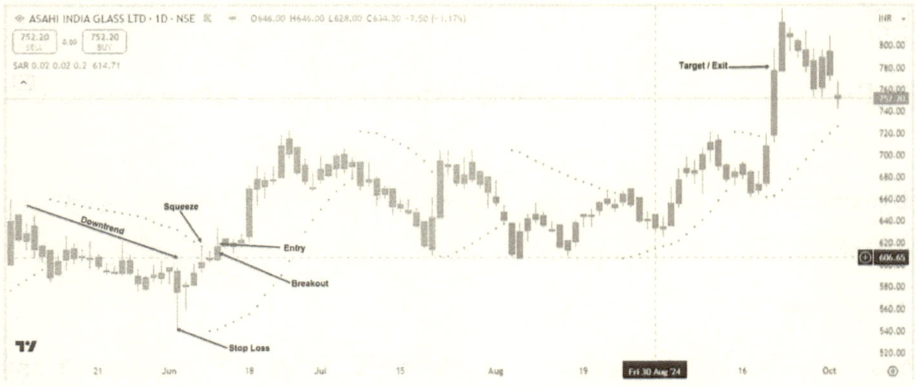

52

Parabolic SAR & Renko Strategy

The Parabolic SAR & Renko Strategy combines two technical analysis tools to identify potential trend reversals and generate trading signals. This strategy benefits beginners by helping filter out market noise and providing precise entry and exit points.

Entry:

Bullish Signal: Enter a long position when a new Green (up) Renko brick forms and the Parabolic SAR dots move below the Price.

Bearish Signal: Enter a short position when a new Red (down) Renko brick forms and the Parabolic SAR dots move above the Price.

Stop Loss:

Stop loss should be based on Parabolic SAR, Support/Resistance, or any other indicator.

Exit Rules:

Profit Target: Your profit target should be based on your risk - reward ratio. It could be a specific percentage gain or the next Support/Resistance.

Trailing Stop: You can trail your stop loss using Parabolic SAR to maximize your profit and ride the full momentum as the price moves in your favor.

Risk Management:

Position Sizing: Determine the appropriate size based on your risk tolerance and account size. You should park only 5% of your Capital at a time.

Risk - Reward Ratio: Ensure that your potential profit is significantly greater than your potential loss for each trade. It would help if you kept your Risk - Reward ratio at least 1:2.

Example:

For a Bullish example, refer to the attached chart of ASHOK LEYLAND Ltd. On 26th April 2024, a Green Renko brick was formed, and the price was trading above the Parabolic SAR. We take entry (buy stock) at 184.00 with a stop loss at 162.00 (Support at the previous swing low) and a Target of 228.00 (R: R 1:2). The Risk: reward achieved is 1:2, and the Target hit on 03rd June 2024 with a 23.91% profit on deployed capital.

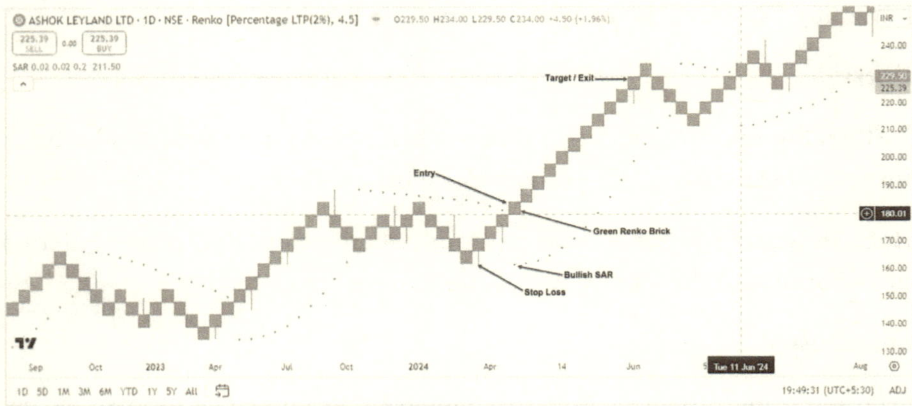

Aroon Indicators

The Aroon indicator is a unique tool for identifying trend strength and reversals. This chapter explores six beginner-friendly strategies. The Aroon Crossover strategy signals trend changes when the up and down lines cross. Use Aroon, SAR & ADX Fusion to combine three indicators for robust trend validation. The Aroon Oscillator simplifies the analysis by highlighting the difference between up and down lines. Learn reversal setups with Aroon & Candlestick Reversal, and refine your trades with Aroon, SAR & Keltner Fusion. The Aroon & Fibonacci Confluence strategy merges Fibonacci retracements with Aroon for high-accuracy setups. Learn how to use Aroon to confirm trends and time your trades with confidence.

53

Aroon Crossover Strategy

The Aroon Crossover is a technical analysis strategy that uses the Aroon indicator to identify potential trend changes and generate trading signals. The Aroon indicator consists of two lines: Aroon Up and Aroon Down. This strategy is beneficial for beginners as it provides clear signals and helps identify the strength of trends.

Entry:

Bullish Signal: Enter a long position when the Aroon Up line crosses above the Aroon Down line, indicating a bullish trend.

Bearish Signal: Enter a short position when the Aroon Down line crosses above the Aroon Up line, signaling a bearish trend.

Stop Loss:

Stop loss should be previous Swing low/high, Support/Resistance, or any other indicator.

Exit Rules:

Profit Target: Your profit target should be based on your risk - reward ratio. It could be a specific percentage gain or the next Support/Resistance.

Trailing Stop: You can trail stop - loss to maximize your profit and ride the full momentum as the price moves in your favor.

Risk Management:

Position Sizing: Determine the appropriate size based on your risk tolerance and account size. You should park only 5% of your Capital at a time.

Risk - Reward Ratio: Ensure that your potential profit is significantly greater than your potential loss for each trade. It would help if you kept your Risk - Reward ratio at least 1:2.

Example:

For a Bullish example, refer to the attached chart of Bajaj Finance. On 23rd August 2024, the Aroon up line crossed over the Aroon down the line, indicating a change in the downtrend, and on 27th August 2024, a green bullish candle with a big body formed. We take entry (buy stock) at 6865.00 with a stop loss at 6420.00 (Previous Swing Low) and a Target of 7760.00 (R: R 1:2). The Risk: Reward achieved is 1:2, and Target hit on 26th September 2024 with 13.04% profit on deployed capital.

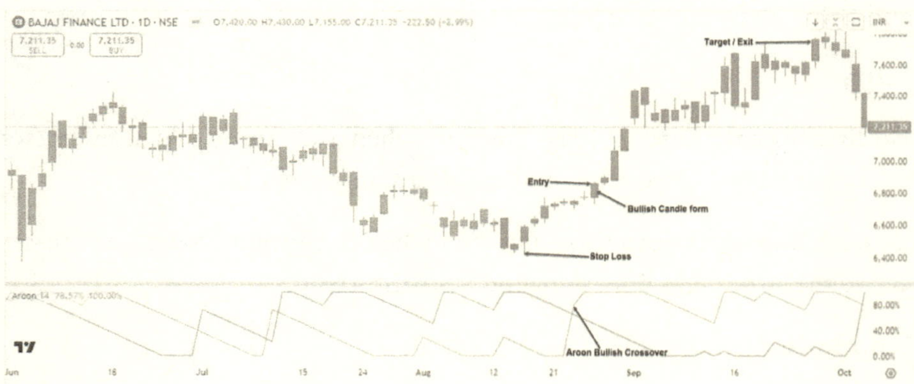

<h1 style="text-align:center">54</h1>

Aroon, SAR & ADX Fusion Strategy

The Aroon, SAR & ADX Fusion strategy combines three technical indicators to identify potential trend reversals and strong trending markets. This approach is designed to provide traders with a more comprehensive view of market dynamics, improving the accuracy of their trading decisions.

Entry:

Bullish Signal: Enter a long position when the Aroon Up > 70 & Aroon Down < 30, SAR dots below Price and ADX > 25.

Bearish Signal: Enter a short position when the Aroon Down > 70 & Aroon Up < 30, SAR dots above Price and ADX<25.

Stop Loss:

Stop loss should be previous Swing low/high, Support/Resistance, or any other indicator.

Exit Rules:

Profit Target: Your profit target should be based on your risk - reward ratio. It could be a specific percentage gain or the next Support/Resistance.

Trailing Stop: You can trail stop - loss to maximize your profit and ride the full momentum as the price moves in your favor.

Risk Management:

Position Sizing: Determine the appropriate size based on your risk tolerance and account size. You should park only 5% of your Capital at a time.

Risk - Reward Ratio: Ensure that your potential profit is significantly greater than your potential loss for each trade. It would help if you kept your Risk - Reward ratio at least 1:2.

Example:

For a Bullish example, refer to the attached chart of AUBANK. On 29[th]August 2024, the Aroon up line> 70, Aroon down line < 30, SAR is trading below Price and ADX > 25. We take entry (buy stock) at 640.00 with a stop loss at 600.00 (Previous Swing Low) and a Target of 720.00 (R: R 1:2). The Risk: Reward achieved is 1:2, and Target hit on 05[th]September 2024 with 12.50% profit on deployed capital.

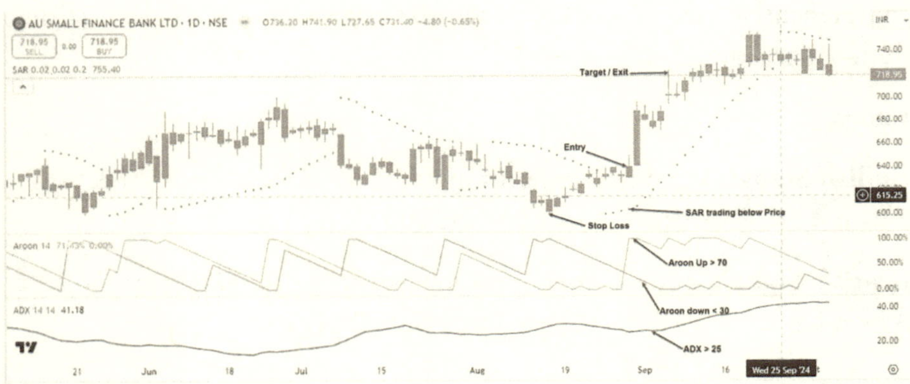

55

Aroon Oscillator Strategy

The Aroon Oscillator is a trend - following indicator that measures the strength of a current trend and the likelihood that it will continue. It's derived from the Aroon Up and Aroon Down indicators and oscillates between- 100 and +100. This method can help traders identify the start of new trends, measure trend strength, and spot potential reversals.

Entry:

Bullish Signal: Enter a long position when the Aroon Oscillator crosses above zero.

Bearish Signal: Enter a short position when the Aroon Oscillator crosses below zero.

Stop Loss:

Stop loss should be previous Swing low/high, Support/Resistance, or any other indicator.

Exit Rules:

Profit Target: Your profit target should be based on your risk - reward ratio. It could be a specific percentage gain or the next Support/Resistance.

Trailing Stop: You can trail stop - loss to maximize your profit and ride the full momentum as the price moves in your favor.

Risk Management:

Position Sizing: Determine the appropriate size based on your risk tolerance and account size. You should park only 5% of your Capital at a time.

Risk - Reward Ratio: Ensure that your potential profit is significantly greater than your potential loss for each trade. It would help if you kept your Risk - Reward ratio at least 1:2.

Example:

For a Bullish example, refer to the attached chart of Astrazeneca Pharma Ltd. On 16th May2024, the Aroon oscillator crosses above zero, and Price breaks out of the previous swing high. We take entry (buy stock) at 5655.00 with a stop loss at 4800.00 (Previous Swing Low) and a Target of 7370.00 (R: R 1:2). The Risk: reward achieved is 1:2, and the Target hit on 04thJuly 2024 with 30.33% profit on deployed capital.

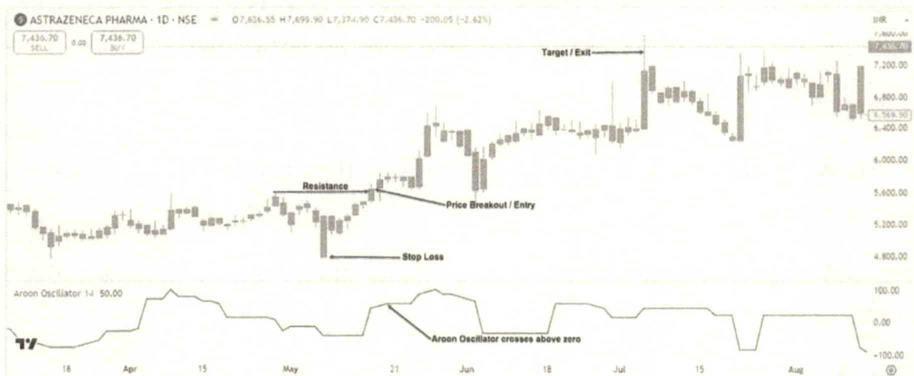

56

Aroon & Candlestick Reversal Strategy

The Aroon & Candlestick Reversal strategy combines the Aroon indicator with candlestick reversal patterns to identify potential trend reversals in the stock market. The Aroon indicator helps detect the strength of a trend, while candlestick patterns provide visual clues for possible reversals. When both signals combine, it can give traders a strong indication of a market turn, making this strategy suitable for both beginners and experienced traders.

Identify the trend: when the Aroon Up is above 70, it indicates a strong uptrend. Similarly, when Aroon Down is above 70, it indicates a strong downtrend. Crossovers between Aroon Up and Aroon Down can signal a trend reversal. Identify Key Candlestick Reversal Patterns: Focus on common reversal patterns like Bullish/Bearish Engulfing, Piercing, Hammer, Hanging man etc.

Entry:

Bullish Signal: Enter a long position when the Aroon up crosses above 70 and bullish candle formation such as Engulfing, Piercing, Hammer, Three White Soldier, etc.

Bearish Signal: Enter a short position when the Aroon down crosses above 70 and bearish candle formation such as Engulfing, Piercing, Hanging Man, Three black crows, etc.

Stop Loss:

Stop loss should be previous Swing low/high, Support/Resistance, or any other indicator.

Exit Rules:

Profit Target: Your profit target should be based on your risk - reward ratio. It could be a specific percentage gain or the next Support/Resistance.

Trailing Stop: You can trail stop - loss to maximize your profit and ride the full momentum as the price moves in your favor.

Risk Management:

Position Sizing: Determine the appropriate size based on your risk tolerance and account size. You should park only 5% of your Capital at a time.

Risk - Reward Ratio: Ensure that your potential profit is significantly greater than your potential loss for each trade. It would help if you kept your Risk - Reward ratio at least 1:2.

Example:

For a Bullish example, refer to the attached chart of Aurobindo Pharma Ltd. On 05[th]July 2024, the Aroon up crosses above Aroon down, indicating a change in trend; the Aroon up crosses above 70, indicating a strong bullish trend, and the Three White Soldier bullish candlesticks pattern forms, confirming the strong bullish trend. We take entry (buy stock) at 1305.00 with a stop loss at 1180.00 (Previous Swing Low) and a Target of 1555.00 (R: R 1:2). The Risk: Reward achieved is 1:2, and Target hit on 27[th]August 2024 with 19.16% profit on deployed capital.

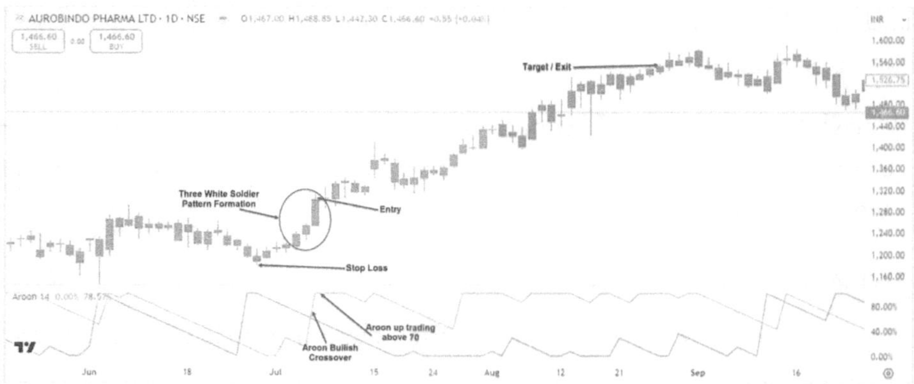

57

Aroon, SAR & Keltner Fusion Strategy

The Aroon, Parabolic SAR, and Keltner Channels fusion strategy combines trend, momentum, and volatility indicators to help traders identify potential entry and exit points more precisely. The Aroon indicator measures the strength and direction of trends, the Parabolic SAR helps determine the direction and likely reversal points, and the Keltner Channels highlight volatility and dynamic support/resistance zones. This strategy is ideal for beginners looking to capture trend - based opportunities in the stock market.

Entry:

Bullish Signal: Enter a long position when (a) Aroon Up should be above 70, indicating a strong uptrend. (b) Parabolic SAR dots trading below the Price, confirming the uptrend, and (c) the price retraces to the middle/lower Keltner band or crosses above the high band.

Bearish Signal: Enter a short position when (a) Aroon Down should be above 70, indicating a strong downtrend. (b) Parabolic SAR dots trading above the Price, confirming the downtrend, and (c) the price retraces to the middle/upper Keltner band or crosses below the lower band.

Stop Loss:

Stop loss should be previous Swing low/high, Support/Resistance, or any other indicator.

Exit Rules:

Profit Target: Your profit target should be based on your risk - reward ratio. It could be a specific percentage gain or the next Support/Resistance.

Trailing Stop: You can trail stop - loss to maximize your profit and ride the full momentum as the price moves in your favor.

Risk Management:

Position Sizing: Determine the appropriate size based on your risk tolerance and account size. You should park only 5% of your Capital at a time.

Risk - Reward Ratio: Ensure that your potential profit is significantly greater than your potential loss for each trade. It would help if you kept your Risk - Reward ratio at least 1:2.

Example:

For a Bullish example, refer to the attached chart of Bajaj Finserv Ltd. On 26th August 2024, the Aroon up crossed above 70, indicating a strong bullish trend; SAR is trading below the Price, confirming the bullish trend. The Price breaks out of the upper band of the Keltner Channel, indicating strong bullish momentum. We take entry (buy stock) at 1685.00 with a stop loss at 1520.00 (Previous Swing Low) and a Target of 2015.00 (R: R 1:2). The Risk: Reward achieved is 1:2, and Target hit on 27[th]September 2024 with 19.58% profit on deployed capital.

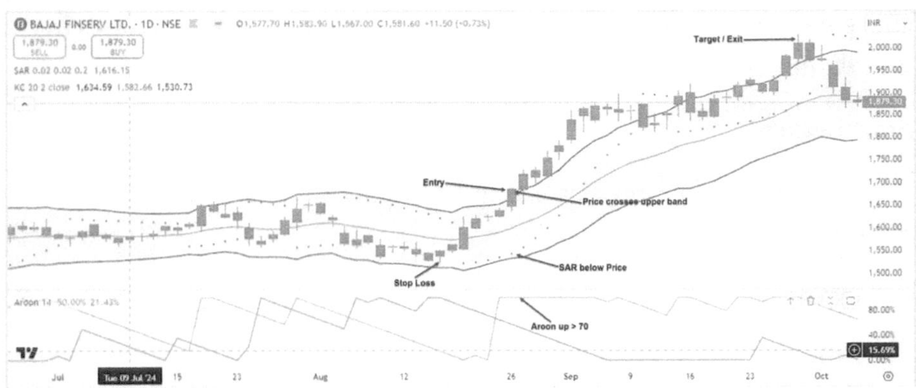

58

Aroon & Fibonacci Confluence Strategy

The Aroon & Fibonacci Confluence Strategy combines the power of the Aroon Indicator with the precision of Fibonacci retracement levels to spot potential trend continuation or reversal points in the market. The Aroon Indicator helps identify the strength of a trend, while Fibonacci retracement levels help pinpoint potential price correction areas where the market might reverse or continue in the prevailing trend. This combination is helpful for traders who want to enter trades with precise entry and exit points while managing risk effectively.

Entry:

Bullish Signal: Enter a long position when the price is in an uptrend and retraces up to critical Fibonacci levels such as 23.6%, 38.2%, 61.8%, 78.6%, etc., bounces back, and Aroon is up > 70.

Bearish Signal: Enter a short position when, in a downtrend, the Price retraces up to critical Fibonacci levels such as 23.6%, 38.2%, 61.8%, 78.6%, etc., bounces back, and Aroon is down > 70.

Stop Loss:

Stop loss should be previous Swing low/high, Support/Resistance, or any other indicator.

Exit Rules:

Profit Target: Your profit target should be based on your risk - reward ratio. It could be a specific percentage gain or the next Support/Resistance.

Trailing Stop: You can trail stop - loss to maximize your profit and ride the full momentum as the price moves in your favor.

Risk Management:

Position Sizing: Determine the appropriate size based on your risk tolerance and account size. You should park only 5% of your Capital at a time.

Risk - Reward Ratio: Ensure that your potential profit is significantly greater than your potential loss for each trade. It would help if you kept your Risk - Reward ratio at least 1:2.

Example:

For a Bullish example, refer to the attached chart of Bajaj Holdings & Inv. Ltd. After making a high on 29[th]February 2024, the price starts retracing & it retraces up to 61.8% Fibonacci levels on 04th June 2024. After retracement, Price bounced back & Aroon up to crosses above 70 on 07th June 2024. We take entry (buy stock) at 8380.00 with a stop loss at 7655.00 (Previous Swing Low) and a Target of 9840.00 (R: R 1:2). The Risk: Reward achieved is 1:2, and Target hit on 04[th]July 2024 with 17.42% profit on deployed capital.

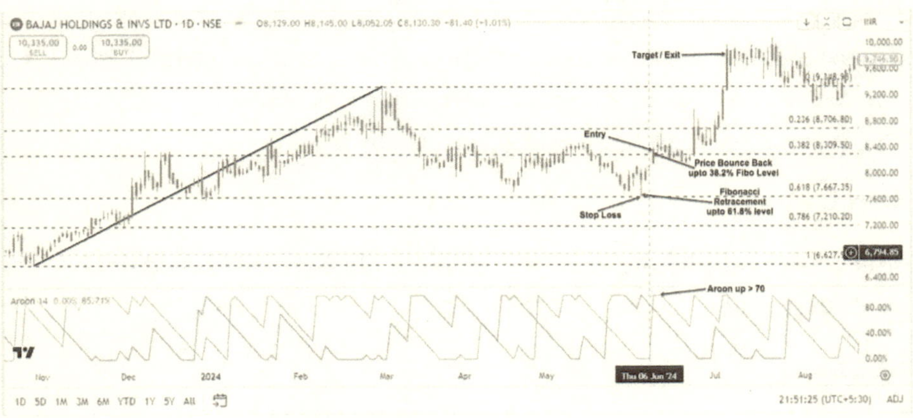

ADX Trend Filters

The ADX (Average Directional Index) helps traders measure trend strength. This chapter introduces five strategies. Start with ADX Trend Identification to filter strong trends from weak ones. The ADX Squeeze & Range Breakout strategy highlights breakout opportunities from consolidations. Use ADX Rainbow Momentum to trade with multiple ADX lines for enhanced accuracy. The ADX MACD Histogram Trades strategy combines ADX with MACD for dual confirmation. Finally, integrate volume analysis with the ADX OBV Money Flow Integration strategy. By mastering these techniques, you'll be able to filter out weak trends and focus on high-probability setups.

59

ADX Trend Identification Strategy

The Average Directional Index (ADX) is a technical indicator used to measure the strength of a trend, regardless of its direction. It helps traders identify strong trends and avoid trading in choppy or sideways markets. The ADX ranges from 0 to 100, with higher values indicating stronger trends.ADX below 25 indicates a Weak or no trend, and ADX above 25 indicates a Moderate to strong trend.

Entry:

Bullish Signal: Enter a long position when the ADX is above 25 and rising in an uptrend. Confirm with Price action, such as a Bullish pattern or Price Breakout.

Bearish Signal: Enter a short position when the ADX is above 25 and rising in a downtrend. Confirm with Price action, such as a Bearish pattern or Price breakdown.

Stop Loss:

Stop loss should be previous Swing low/high, Support/Resistance, or any other indicator.

Exit Rules:

Profit Target: Your profit target should be based on your risk - reward ratio. It could be a specific percentage gain or the next Support/Resistance.

Trailing Stop: You can trail stop - loss to maximize your profit and ride the full momentum as the price moves in your favor.

Risk Management:

Position Sizing: Determine the appropriate size based on your risk tolerance and account size. You should park only 5% of your Capital at a time.

Risk - Reward Ratio: Ensure that your potential profit is significantly greater than your potential loss for each trade. It would help if you kept your Risk - Reward ratio at least 1:2.

Example:

For a Bullish example, refer to the attached chart of Bajaj Auto Ltd. After a long consolidation, the Price starts moving up, and the ADX crosses over 25 on 11th April 2023. The Price is also trading above the previous swing high. We take entry (buy stock) at 4180.00 with a stop loss at 3765.00 (Previous Swing Low) and a Target of 5010.00 (R: R 1:2). The Risk: reward achieved is 1:2, and the Target hit on 15th September 2023 with a 19.86% profit on deployed capital.

60

ADX Squeeze & Range Breakout Strategy

The ADX Squeeze & Range Breakout Strategy combines two powerful tools in technical analysis: the Average Directional Index (ADX), which measures trend strength, and the Bollinger Bands Squeeze, which identifies periods of low volatility that often precede large price movements. This strategy helps traders to spot breakouts after consolidation phases, where prices are typically "squeezed" into a narrow range.

Entry:

Bullish Signal: Enter a long position after the Bollinger Band squeeze. Price breaks out of the upper band, and the ADX is above 25 and rising.

Bearish Signal: Enter a short position after the Bollinger Band squeeze. The price breaks down the lower band, and the ADX is above 25 and rising.

Stop Loss:

Stop loss should be previous Swing low/high, Support/Resistance, or any other indicator.

Exit Rules:

Profit Target: Your profit target should be based on your risk - reward ratio. It could be a specific percentage gain or the next Support/Resistance.

Trailing Stop: You can trail stop - loss to maximize your profit and ride the full momentum as the price moves in your favor.

Risk Management:

Position Sizing: Determine the appropriate size based on your risk tolerance and account size. You should park only 5% of your Capital at a time.

Risk - Reward Ratio: Ensure that your potential profit is significantly greater than your potential loss for each trade. It would help if you kept your Risk - Reward ratio at least 1:2.

Example:

For a bullish example, refer to the attached chart of Bharat Electronics Ltd. After a squeeze, the price broke out in the upper band of the Bollinger band on 06th December 2023, and ADX is also trading above 25 and rising. We take entry (buy stock) at 156.00 with a stop loss at 137.00 (Previous Swing Low) and a Target of 194.00 (R: R 1:2). The Risk: reward achieved is 1:2, and the Target hit on 20th January 2024 with 24.36% profit on deployed capital.

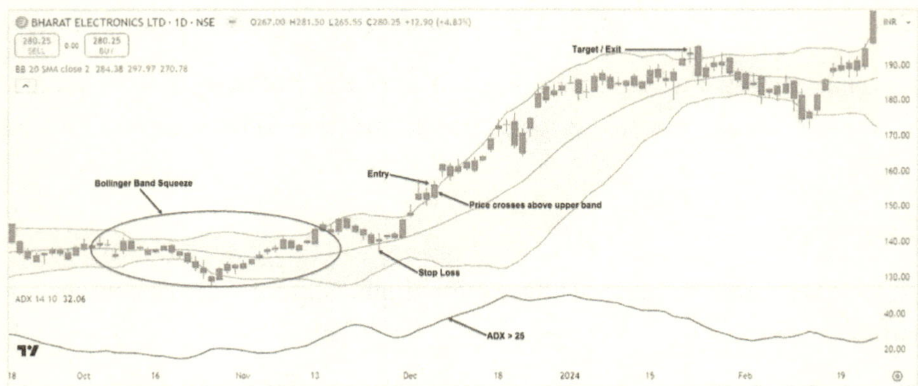

61

ADX Rainbow Momentum Strategy

The ADX Rainbow Momentum strategy combines the Average Directional Index (ADX) indicator with multiple Exponential Moving Averages (EMAs) to identify trending markets and potential entry points. This strategy captures strong trends while filtering out sideways or choppy market conditions.

Entry:

Bullish Signal: Enter a long position when ADX > 25, EMAs are aligned bullishly, i.e., shorter EMAs trade above longer EMAs, and Price closes above all EMAs.

Bearish Signal: Enter a short position when ADX > 25, EMAs aligned bearishly, i.e., shorter EMA trading below longer EMA, and Price closes below all EMAs.

Stop Loss:

Stop loss should be previous Swing low/high, Support/Resistance, or any other indicator.

Exit Rules:

Profit Target: Your profit target should be based on your risk - reward ratio. It could be a specific percentage gain or the next Support/Resistance.

Trailing Stop: You can trail stop - loss to maximize your profit and ride the full momentum as the price moves in your favor.

Risk Management:

Position Sizing: Determine the appropriate size based on your risk tolerance and account size. You should park only 5% of your Capital at a time.

Risk - Reward Ratio: Ensure that your potential profit is significantly greater than your potential loss for each trade. It would help if you kept your Risk - Reward ratio at least 1:2.

Example:

For a Bullish example, refer attached chart of Bosch Ltd. On 23rd November 2023, ADX > 25, 5EMA > 20EMA > 50EMA > 100EMA, and Price breaks out the previous swing high. We take entry (buy stock) at 21210.00 with a stop loss at 19300.00 (Previous Swing Low) and a Target of 25050.00 (R: R 1:2). The Risk: Reward achieved is 1:2, and Target hit on 07[th]February 2024 with 18.10% profit on deployed capital.

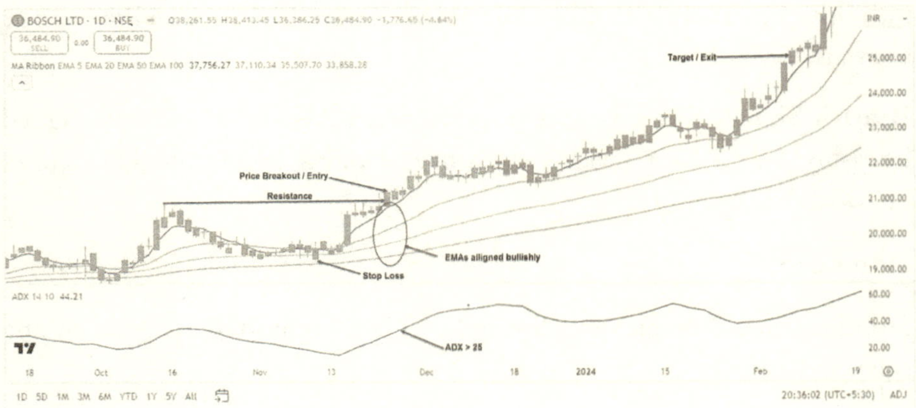

62

ADX MACD Histogram Trade Strategy

The ADX MACD Histogram Trade strategy combines the Average Directional Index (ADX) with the Moving Average Convergence Divergence (MACD) Histogram to identify strong trends and potential entry points. This strategy aims to capture high - probability trades by confirming trend strength and momentum.

Entry:

Bullish Signal: Enter a long position when ADX > 25, the MACD line crosses above the signal line, and the MACD Histogram turns positive.

Bearish Signal: Enter a short position when ADX > 25, the MACD line crosses below the signal line, and the MACD Histogram turns negative.

Stop Loss:

Stop loss should be previous Swing low/high, Support/Resistance, or any other indicator.

Exit Rules:

Profit Target: Your profit target should be based on your risk - reward ratio. It could be a specific percentage gain or the next Support/Resistance.

Trailing Stop: You can trail stop - loss to maximize your profit and ride the full momentum as the price moves in your favor.

Risk Management:

Position Sizing: Determine the appropriate size based on your risk tolerance and account size. You should park only 5% of your Capital at a time.

Risk - Reward Ratio: Ensure that your potential profit is significantly greater than your potential loss for each trade. It would help if you kept your Risk - Reward ratio at least 1:2.

Example:

For a Bullish example, refer to the attached chart of Brigade Enter. Ltd. On 03rd November 2023, ADX > 25, MACD is trading above the signal line, the MACD Histogram is positive (Dark Green), and the Price breaks out of the previous swing high. We take entry (buy stock) at 668.00 with a stop loss at 580.00 (Previous Swing Low) and a Target of 845.00 (R: R 1:2). The Risk: reward achieved is 1:2, and the Target hit on 01st December 2023 with a 26.50% profit on deployed capital.

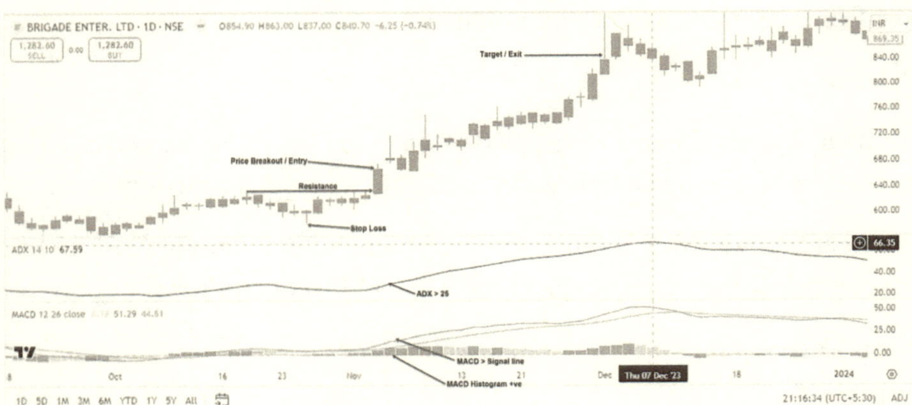

63

ADX OBV Money Flow Integration Strategy

The ADX (Average Directional Index), OBV (On - Balance Volume), and Money Flow Integration are powerful technical analysis techniques that help traders identify trends and confirm market momentum in the Indian stock market. By combining these three indicators, traders may gain a better understanding of the underlying market dynamics and make better trading decisions.

Entry:

Bullish Signal: Enter a long position when ADX > 25, OBV is rising, and MFI is rising &> 50.

Bearish Signal: Enter a short position when ADX > 25, OBV is falling, and MFI is falling &< 50.

Stop Loss:

Stop loss should be previous Swing low/high, Support/Resistance, or any other indicator.

Exit Rules:

Profit Target: Your profit target should be based on your risk - reward ratio. It could be a specific percentage gain or the next Support/Resistance.

Trailing Stop: You can trail stop - loss to maximize your profit and ride the full momentum as the price moves in your favor.

Risk Management:

Position Sizing: Determine the appropriate size based on your risk tolerance and account size. You should park only 5% of your Capital at a time.

Risk - Reward Ratio: Ensure that your potential profit is significantly greater than your potential loss for each trade. It would help if you kept your Risk - Reward ratio at least 1:2.

Example:

For a Bullish example, refer to the attached chart of Britannia Industries Ltd. After a downtrend price reverse, on 07th May 2024, ADX > 25, OBV is rising, and MFI is rising &> 50. We take entry (buy stock) at 5175.00 with a stop loss at 4700.00 (Previous Swing Low) and a Target of 6125.00 (R: R 1:2). The Risk: reward achieved is 1:2, and the Target hit on 12th September 2024 with an 18.36% profit on deployed capital.

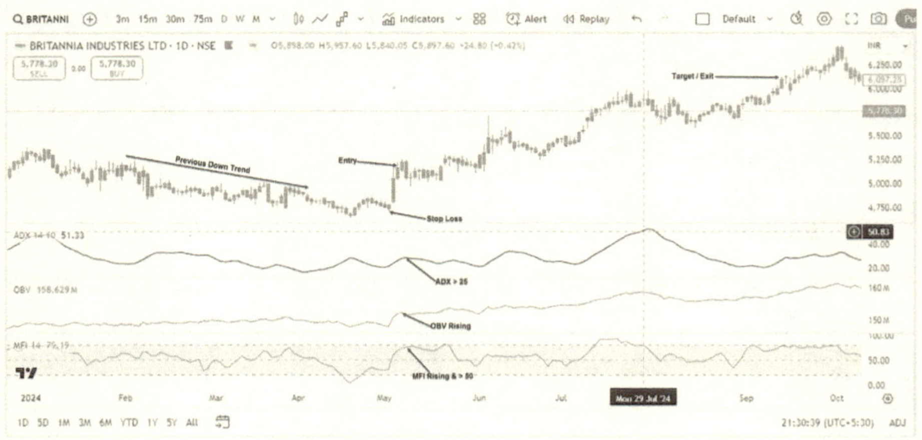

OBV Momentum

On-Balance Volume (OBV) is a cornerstone indicator in the world of technical analysis, serving as a bridge between price movements and trading volume. This chapter unpacks OBV's fundamental role in tracking the flow of volume to predict market trends. By understanding OBV, traders can decode how institutional investors drive prices by observing volume shifts.

The chapter introduces OBV as a running total of volume that adds or subtracts depending on whether the closing price moves up or down. It explains how sharp rises or falls in OBV often precede corresponding moves in price, allowing traders to anticipate market trends with precision. Additionally, the chapter dives into how divergences between OBV and price can reveal hidden shifts in momentum, offering critical early signals of potential reversals. Through clear examples and actionable insights, beginners will learn how to integrate OBV into their trading strategies to enhance decision-making and confirm breakout opportunities.

64

OBV (On – Balance Volume) Breakout Strategy

The OBV indicator confirms trends by analyzing volume flow. A breakout in OBV indicates high - volume trading; therefore, high momentum is expected after the breakout.

Entry:

Bullish Signal: Enter a long position when the OBV line breaks out after a long consolidation and there is price action, indicating bullish volume confirmation and potential trend continuation.

Bearish Signal: Enter a short position when the OBV line breaks down after a long consolidation, and there is price action, signaling bearish volume confirmation and potential trend continuation.

Stop Loss:

Stop loss should be previous Swing low/high, Support/Resistance, or any other indicator.

Exit Rules:

Profit Target: Your profit target should be based on your risk - reward ratio. It could be a specific percentage gain or the next Support/Resistance.

Trailing Stop: You can trail stop - loss to maximize your profit and ride the full momentum as the price moves in your favor.

Risk Management:

Position Sizing: Determine the appropriate size based on your risk tolerance and account size. You should park only 5% of your Capital at a time.

Risk - Reward Ratio: Ensure that your potential profit is significantly greater than your potential loss for each trade. It would help if you kept your Risk - Reward ratio at least 1:2.

Example:

For a Bullish example, refer to the attached chart of Ashok Leyland. On 26[th]April 2024, the OBV gives a breakout after a long consolidation; Price provides a breakout with and crosses above the previous swing high. We take entry (buy stock) at 185.00 with a stop loss at 165.00 (Previous swing low) and a Target of 225.00 (R: R 1:2). The Risk: Reward achieved is 1:2, and the Target hit on 27th May2024 with 21.62% profit on deployed capital.

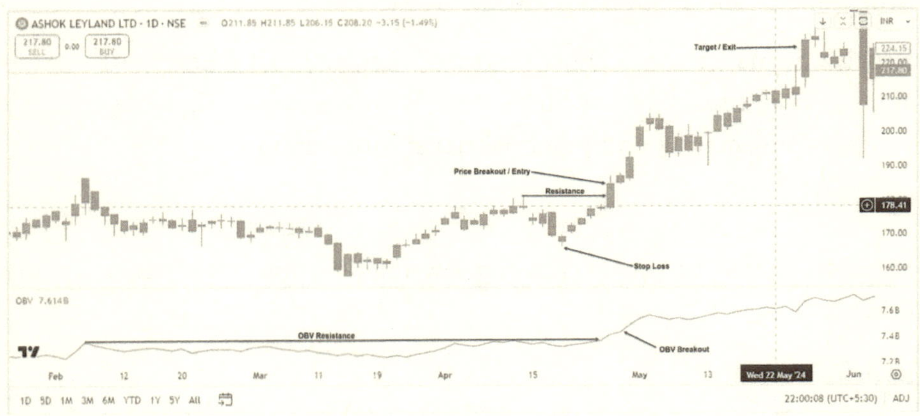

65

OBV Momentum Divergences Strategy

The on - balance volume (OBV) is a momentum indicator that measures volume flow to predict price changes. It assumes that volume precedes price movement, meaning when volume increases significantly without a corresponding price increase, the Price is likely to follow. OBV divergences, particularly with price momentum, occur when the price moves in one direction, but OBV moves in the opposite direction. This divergence can signal a potential reversal of the trend.

Entry:

Bullish Signal: Enter a long position when the bullish divergence occurs, i.e., Price will form lower lows, while OBV will form higher lows.

Bearish Signal: Enter a short position when the bearish divergence occurs. Price will form higher highs, while OBV will form lower highs.

Stop Loss:

Stop loss should be previous Swing low/high, Support/Resistance, or any other indicator.

Exit Rules:

Profit Target: Your profit target should be based on your risk - reward ratio. It could be a specific percentage gain or the next Support/Resistance.

Trailing Stop: You can trail stop - loss to maximize your profit and ride the full momentum as the price moves in your favor.

Risk Management:

Position Sizing: Determine the appropriate size based on your risk tolerance and account size. You should park only 5% of your Capital at a time.

Risk - Reward Ratio: Ensure that your potential profit is significantly greater than your potential loss for each trade. It would help if you kept your Risk - Reward ratio at least 1:2.

Example:

For a Bullish example, refer to the attached chart of Century Ply Ltd. In Mar 2024, last week, a bullish diversion occurred as OBV made higher lows whereas Price made lower lows. After diversion, a bullish candle with a strong body formed on 04[th]April 2024. We take entry (buy stock) at 670.00 with a stop loss at 622.00 (Previous swing low) and a Target of 766.00 (R: R 1:2). The Risk: Reward achieved is 1:2, and Target hit on 28th June 2024 with 14.33% profit on deployed capital.

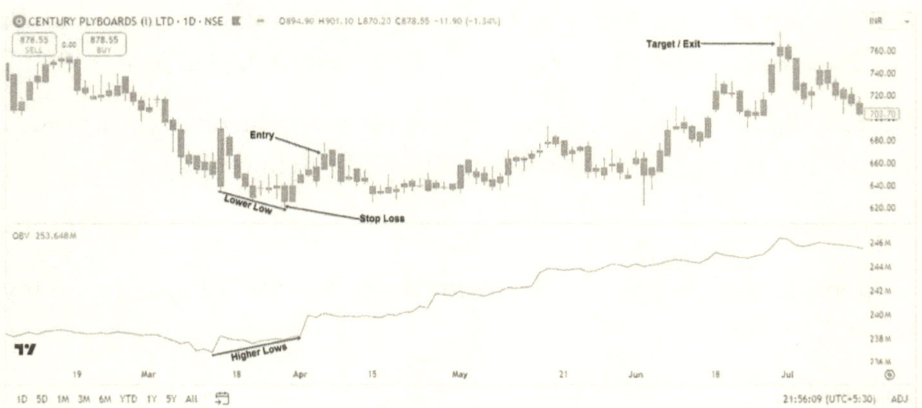

66

OBV Squeeze & Breakout Strategy

The OBV (On - Balance Volume) Squeeze and breakout strategy is based on the idea that Price consolidates before a significant move. This period of low volatility can be seen on the OBV indicator, forming a "squeeze" phase. Once the Price breaks out of this consolidation, accompanied by a sharp rise in OBV, it signals a potentially significant price movement. The OBV helps confirm the breakout's direction, as a volume surge typically supports the upcoming trend.

Entry:

Bullish Signal: Enter a long position when the price moves above resistance and OBV spikes upward, showing buyers are aggressively entering the market.

Bearish Signal: Enter a short position when the price breaks below support and OBV drops sharply, signaling heavy selling pressure.

Stop Loss:

Stop loss should be previous Swing low/high, Support/Resistance, or any other indicator.

Exit Rules:

Profit Target: Your profit target should be based on your risk - reward ratio. It could be a specific percentage gain or the next Support/Resistance.

Trailing Stop: You can trail stop - loss to maximize your profit and ride the full momentum as the price moves in your favor.

Risk Management:

Position Sizing: Determine the appropriate size based on your risk tolerance and account size. You should park only 5% of your Capital at a time.

Risk - Reward Ratio: Ensure that your potential profit is significantly greater than your potential loss for each trade. It would help if you kept your Risk - Reward ratio at least 1:2.

Example:

For a Bullish example, refer to the attached chart of Caplin Point Lab Ltd. After a long consolidation of over two months; Price broke out of previous resistance along with a good spike in OBV on 10[th]June 2024. We take entry (buy stock) at 1476.00 with a stop loss at 1225.00 (Previous swing low) and a Target of 1980.00 (R: R 1:2). The Risk: reward achieved is 1:2, and the Target hit on 27[th]August 2024 with 34.15% profit on deployed capital.

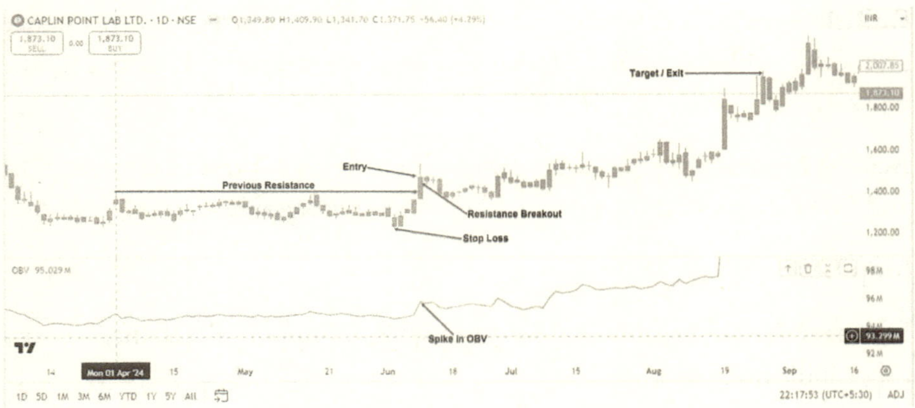

67

OBV ADX Trend Confirmation Strategy

The OBV (On - Balance Volume) and ADX (Average Directional Index) indicators are powerful tools for identifying and confirming trends in the stock market. OBV measures buying and selling pressure by calculating cumulative volume, while ADX quantifies the strength of a trend. They can help traders spot and confirm bullish or bearish trends when used together.

Entry:

Bullish Signal: Enter a long position when OBV rises along with Price and ADX > 25.

Bearish Signal: Enter a short position when OBV falls along with Price and ADX > 25.

Stop Loss:

Stop loss should be previous Swing low/high, Support/Resistance, or any other indicator.

Exit Rules:

Profit Target: Your profit target should be based on your risk - reward ratio. It could be a specific percentage gain or the next Support/Resistance.

Trailing Stop: You can trail stop - loss to maximize your profit and ride the full momentum as the price moves in your favor.

Risk Management:

Position Sizing: Determine the appropriate size based on your risk tolerance and account size. You should park only 5% of your Capital at a time.

Risk - Reward Ratio: Ensure that your potential profit is significantly greater than your potential loss for each trade. It would help if you kept your Risk - Reward ratio at least 1:2.

Example:

For a Bullish example, refer to the attached chart of BSE Ltd. On 16th September 24, ADX > 25, there is a spike in OBV and a bullish green candle with prominent body forms. We take entry (buy stock) at 3430.00 with a stop loss at 2700.00 (Previous swing low) and a Target of 4900.00 (R: R 1:2). The Risk: reward achieved is 1:2, and the Target hit on 14th October 2024 with 42.86% profit on deployed capital.

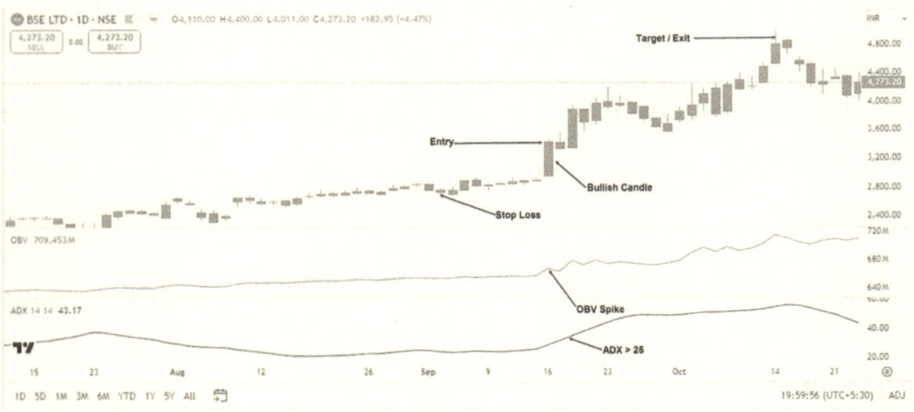

Keltner Channels

Keltner Channels are a technical analysis tool that blends moving averages with volatility measures, creating a dynamic framework for identifying trading opportunities. This chapter demystifies the concept of Keltner Channels, illustrating how they are constructed using an exponential moving average (EMA) and a multiple of the Average True Range (ATR).

Readers will explore the versatility of Keltner Channels in various market conditions, from trend-following strategies during strong movements to range-trading approaches in consolidating markets. The chapter emphasizes how the channel boundaries act as dynamic support and resistance levels, helping traders determine overbought or oversold conditions. Beginners will also learn how to interpret price interactions with the channel, such as breakouts and reversals, to pinpoint high-probability trade setups. With practical guidance, this chapter equips traders with a reliable tool for managing risk and enhancing trade timing.

68

Standard Keltner Channel Strategy

Keltner Channels is a volatility - based indicator consisting of an exponential moving average (EMA) and upper and lower bands based on the average true range (ATR).It helps traders identify overbought and oversold zones, potential breakouts or trend reversals, and trend - following and reversal strategies. One can also use Keltner Channels to confirm other technical signals.

Entry:

Bullish Signal: Enter a long position when the Price breaks out above the upper Keltner Channel, indicating a bullish breakout.

Bearish Signal: Enter a short position when the Price breaks below the lower Keltner Channel, signaling a bearish breakout.

Stop Loss:

The Stop loss should be the mid - line of the Keltner Channel at buying time, Support/Resistance, or any other indicator.

Exit Rules:

Profit Target: Your profit target should be based on your risk - reward ratio. It could be a specific percentage gain or the next Support/Resistance.

Trailing Stop: You can trail stop - loss to maximize your profit and ride the full momentum as the price moves in your favor.

Risk Management:

Position Sizing: Determine the appropriate size based on your risk tolerance and account size. You should park only 5% of your Capital at a time.

Risk - Reward Ratio: Ensure that your potential profit is significantly greater than your potential loss for each trade. It would help if you kept your Risk - Reward ratio at least 1:2.

Example:

For a Bullish example, refer to the attached chart of HDFC Bank Ltd. On 04[th]April 2024, the Price breaks out of the Keltner Channel upper line. We take entry (buy stock) at 1530.00 with a stop loss at 1420.00 (Previous swing low) and a Target of 1750.00 (R: R 1:2). The Risk: reward achieved is 1:2, and the Target hit on 03rd July 2024 with 14.38% profit on deployed capital.

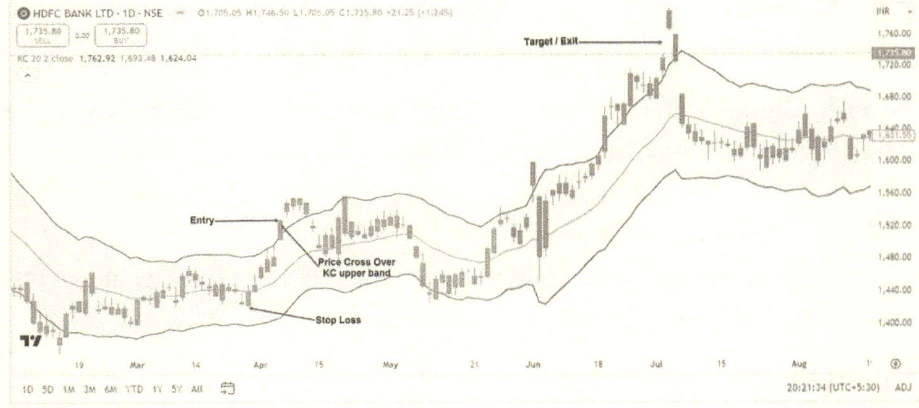

69

Keltner, MACD & RSI Confluence Strategy

The Keltner Channel, MACD & RSI Confluence Strategy is a popular method that combines three indicators: Keltner Channels for trend direction, MACD (Moving Average Convergence Divergence) for momentum and trend strength, and RSI (Relative Strength Index) for overbought/oversold conditions. By using the confluence of these indicators, traders can better identify high - probability trade setups.

Entry:

Bullish Signal: Enter a long position when the Price crosses above the Keltner Channel upper band (uptrend), the MACD line crosses/trades above the signal line, and the RSI is> 50 and rising.

Bearish Signal: Enter a short position when the Price crosses below the Keltner Channel lower band (downtrend), the MACD line crosses/trades below the signal line, and RSI < 50 &is declining.

Stop Loss:

The Stop loss should be the mid - line of the Keltner Channel at buying time, Support/Resistance, or any other indicator.

Exit Rules:

Profit Target: Your profit target should be based on your risk - reward ratio. It could be a specific percentage gain or the next Support/Resistance.

Trailing Stop: You can trail stop - loss to maximize your profit and ride the full momentum as the price moves in your favor.

Risk Management:

Position Sizing: Determine the appropriate size based on your risk tolerance and account size. You should park only 5% of your Capital at a time.

Risk - Reward Ratio: Ensure that your potential profit is significantly greater than your potential loss for each trade. It would help if you kept your Risk - Reward ratio at least 1:2.

Example:

For a Bullish example, refer to the attached chart of Infosys Ltd. On 07th June 2024, the Price breaks out the Keltner Channel upper line, MACD trades above the signal line, and RSI > 50. We take entry (buy stock) at 1535.00 with a stop loss at 1355.00 (Previous swing low) and a Target of 1895.00 (R: R 1:2). The Risk: reward achieved is 1:2, and the Target hit on 29th July 2024 with 23.45% profit on deployed capital.

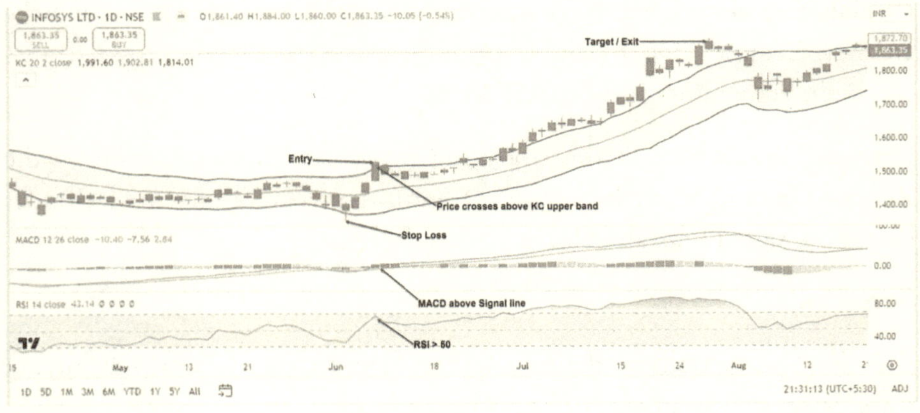

70

Keltner OBV Money Flow Strategy

The Keltner OBV (On - Balance Volume) Money Flow Strategy is a technical trading strategy that combines the Keltner Channel for identifying price trends, OBV for volume - based momentum, and Money Flow Index (MFI) for gauging the strength of money flowing into or out of an asset. This confluence helps traders spot high - probability entries based on Price, volume, and money flow.

Entry:

Bullish Signal: Enter a long position when the Price crosses above the upper Keltner channel band. OBV is rising, indicating increasing volume with the trend. MFI is trading below 80 but rising, confirming that buying pressure is not yet overextended.

Bearish Signal: Enter a short position when the Price crosses below the Keltner Channel lower band. OBV is declining, indicating decreasing volume with the trend, and MFI is trading below 20 but falling, indicating money is flowing out of the stock.

Stop Loss:

The Stop loss should be a mid - line of the Keltner Channel at buying time, Support/Resistance, or any other indicator.

Exit Rules:

Profit Target: Your profit target should be based on your risk - reward ratio. It could be a specific percentage gain or the next Support/Resistance.

Trailing Stop: You can trail stop - loss to maximize your profit and ride the full momentum as the price moves in your favor.

Risk Management:

Position Sizing: Determine the appropriate size based on your risk tolerance and account size. You should park only 5% of your Capital at a time.

Risk - Reward Ratio: Ensure that your potential profit is significantly greater than your potential loss for each trade. It would help if you kept your Risk - Reward ratio at least 1:2.

Example:

For a Bullish example, refer to the attached chart of CAMS Ltd. On 23rd May2024, the Price breaks out the Keltner Channel upper line. OBV is rising, and MFI is below 80 but rising. We take entry (buy stock) at 3550.00 with a stop loss at 3030.00 (Previous swing low) and a Target of 4600.00 (R: R 1:2). The Risk: reward achieved is 1:2, and the Target hit on 30th July 2024 with a 29.58% profit on deployed capital.

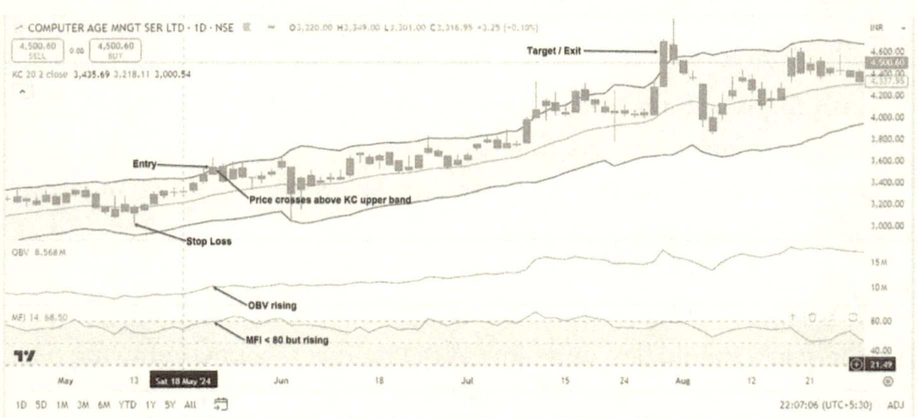

Chande Calculations

The Chande Momentum Oscillator (CMO) is an advanced momentum indicator that provides traders with nuanced insights into market strength and direction. This chapter introduces CMO as a tool for quantifying the intensity of price movements, offering a fresh perspective compared to traditional oscillators like RSI or Stochastics.

The chapter explores how CMO measures momentum by calculating the difference between gains and losses over a specified period, making it highly sensitive to price changes. Readers will discover how to use CMO to identify overbought and oversold conditions, spot potential reversals, and filter out false signals.

Additionally, the chapter highlights the synergy between CMO and other indicators, such as MACD and OBV, for enhanced accuracy in trading decisions. By the end of the chapter, beginners will have a thorough understanding of how to incorporate CMO into their analysis, allowing them to anticipate market moves with confidence and precision.

71

Chande Momentum Oscillator (CMO) Strategy

Chande Momentum Oscillator (CMO) is used to identify overbought and oversold zones and potential trend reversals. CMO signals can be combined with other technical indicators or price patterns to confirm and avoid false signals.

Entry:

Bullish Signal: Enter a long position when the CMO crosses above 0, indicating a potential bullish reversal.

Bearish Signal: Enter a short position when the CMO crosses below 0, signaling a potential bearish reversal.

Stop Loss:

Stop loss should be previous Swing low/high, Support/Resistance, or any other indicator.

Exit Rules:

Profit Target: Your profit target should be based on your risk - reward ratio. It could be a specific percentage gain or the next Support/Resistance.

Trailing Stop: You can trail stop - loss to maximize your profit and ride the full momentum as the price moves in your favor.

Risk Management:

Position Sizing: Determine the appropriate size based on your risk tolerance and account size. You should park only 5% of your Capital at a time.

Risk - Reward Ratio: Ensure that your potential profit is significantly greater than your potential loss for each trade. It would help if you kept your Risk - Reward ratio at least 1:2.

Example:

For a Bullish example, refer to the attached chart of Ashok Leyland. On 26[th]April 2024, the CMO crosses above 0, and the Price breaks out of the previous swing high. We take entry (buy stock) at 185.00 with a stop loss at 165.00 (Previous swing low) and a Target of 225.00 (R: R 1:2). The Risk: reward achieved is 1:2, and the Target hit on 27[th]May2024 with 21.62% profit on deployed capital.

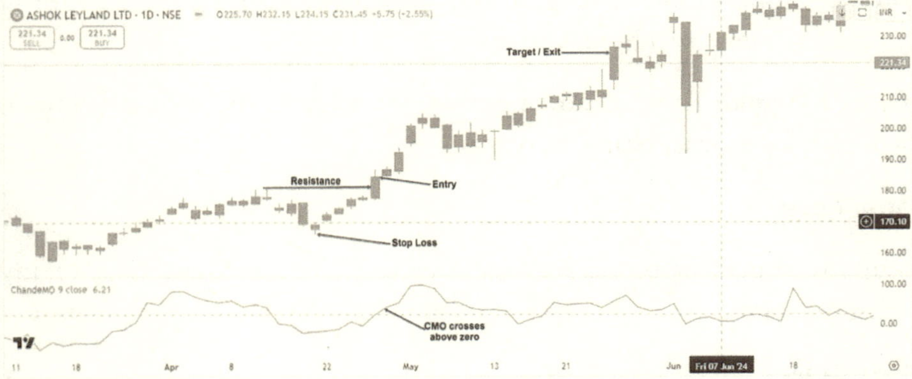

72

Chande Momentum Oscillator, MACD Combo Signals Strategy

The Chande Momentum Oscillator (CMO) and MACD (Moving Average Convergence Divergence) are powerful momentum indicators that complement each other. The CMO helps gauge overbought/oversold conditions, while the MACD identifies trend strength and direction. Combining these tools allows traders to generate reliable entry and exit signals.

Entry:

Bullish Signal: Enter a long position when the CMO rises above- 50, indicating momentum improvement & the MACD line crosses above the signal line. Confirm rising histogram bars for additional bullish confirmation.

Bearish Signal: Enter a short position when the CMO falls below +50, signaling weakening momentum & the MACD line crosses below the signal line. Confirm falling histogram bars for bearish confirmation.

Stop Loss:

Stop loss should be previous Swing Low/High, Support/Resistance, or any other indicator - based.

Exit Rules:

Profit Target: Your profit target should be based on your risk - reward ratio. It could be a specific percentage gain or the next Support/Resistance.

Trailing Stop: You can trail stop - loss to maximize your profit and ride the full momentum as the price moves in your favor.

Risk Management:

Position Sizing: Determine the appropriate size based on your risk tolerance and account size. You should park only 5% of your Capital at a time.

Risk - Reward Ratio: Ensure that your potential profit is significantly greater than your potential loss for each trade. It would help if you kept your Risk - Reward ratio at least 1:2.

Example:

For a Bullish example, refer to the attached chart of EIDPARRY (I) Ltd. CMO of the stock was trading below- 50 between 12th and 20th March 2024. On 02nd April 2024, the CMO was trading above- 50, the MACD line crossed above the Signal line, and Price closed above the previous swing high. We take entry (buy stock) at 583.00 with a stop loss at 539.00 (Previous swing low) and a Target of 671.00 (R: R 1:2). The Risk: Reward achieved is 1:2, and the Target hit on 29[th]May2024 with 15.09% profit on deployed capital.

73

CMO Divergence Strategy

The Chande Momentum Oscillator (CMO) is a momentum - based indicator oscillating between +100 and - 100, reflecting market strength. Using divergence analysis with the CMO can help traders identify potential reversals when price action and the oscillator diverge. This approach is simple yet powerful for spotting turning points in trends.

Bullish Divergence: Price forms lower lows, but the CMO forms higher lows, indicating weakening bearish momentum and a potential upward reversal.

Bearish Divergence: Price forms higher highs, but the CMO forms lower highs, indicating weakening bullish momentum and a potential downward reversal.

Entry:

Bullish Signal: Enter a long position after bullish divergence, i.e., the Price makes lower lows, but the CMO makes higher lows.CMO rises above - 50, confirmed with bullish price action, i.e., a breakout of the previous swing high/resistance.

Bearish Signal: Enter a short position after bearish divergence, i.e., the Price makes higher highs, but the CMO makes lower highs. CMO falls below +50, confirmed with bearish price action, i.e., breakdown of previous swing low/support.

Stop Loss:

Stop loss should be previous Swing Low/High, Support/Resistance, or any other indicator - based.

Exit Rules:

Profit Target: Your profit target should be based on your risk - reward ratio. It could be a specific percentage gain or the next Support/Resistance.

Trailing Stop: You can trail stop - loss to maximize your profit and ride the full momentum as the price moves in your favor.

Risk Management:

Position Sizing: Determine the appropriate size based on your risk tolerance and account size. You should park only 5% of your Capital at a time.

Risk - Reward Ratio: Ensure that your potential profit is significantly greater than your potential loss for each trade. It would help if you kept your Risk - Reward ratio at least 1:2.

Example:

For a bullish example, refer to the attached chart for Deepak Fertilizers. Between 14[th]February and 13th March 2024, a Bullish divergence forms as the price makes lower lows, but the CMO makes higher lows. After bullish divergence on 03[rd]April 2024, the CMO is trading above - 50, and the Price also closes above the previous swing high. We take entry (buy stock) at 557.00 with a stop loss at 450.00 (Previous swing low) and a Target of 771.00 (R: R 1:2). The Risk: Reward achieved is 1:2, and Target hit on 05[th]July 2024 with 38.42% profit on deployed capital.

74

CMO OBV Strategy

The Chande Momentum Oscillator (CMO) is a technical indicator that helps traders to identify overbought or oversold zones. It measures price momentum by comparing recent gains to recent losses. The on - balance volume (OBV) uses volume flow to predict changes in stock price. Combining these indicators allows traders to validate momentum signals with volume trends for improved accuracy.

Entry:

Bullish Signal: Enter a long position when CMO exceeds 30 and OBV rises. Confirm with bullish price action, i.e., a breakout of the previous swing high/resistance.

Bearish Signal: Enter a short position when CMO crosses below- 30 & OBV is falling. Confirm with bearish price action, i.e., previous swing low/ support breakdown.

Stop Loss:

Stop loss should be previous Swing Low/High, Support/Resistance, or any other indicator - based.

Exit Rules:

Profit Target: Your profit target should be based on your risk - reward ratio. It could be a specific percentage gain or the next Support/Resistance.

Trailing Stop: You can trail stop - loss to maximize your profit and ride the full momentum as the price moves in your favor.

Risk Management:

Position Sizing: Determine the appropriate size based on your risk tolerance and account size. You should park only 5% of your Capital at a time.

Risk - Reward Ratio: Ensure that your potential profit is significantly greater than your potential loss for each trade. It would help if you kept your Risk - Reward ratio at least 1:2.

Example:

For a Bullish example, refer to the attached chart of DIVISLAB. On 04th April 2024, the CMO crossed above +30, OBV rose, and the price rose above the previous swing high. We take entry (buy stock) at 3730.00 with a stop loss at 3350.00 (Previous swing low) and a Target of 4500.00 (R: R 1:2). The Risk: reward achieved is 1:2, and the Target hit on 05th June 2024 with 20.64% profit on deployed capital.

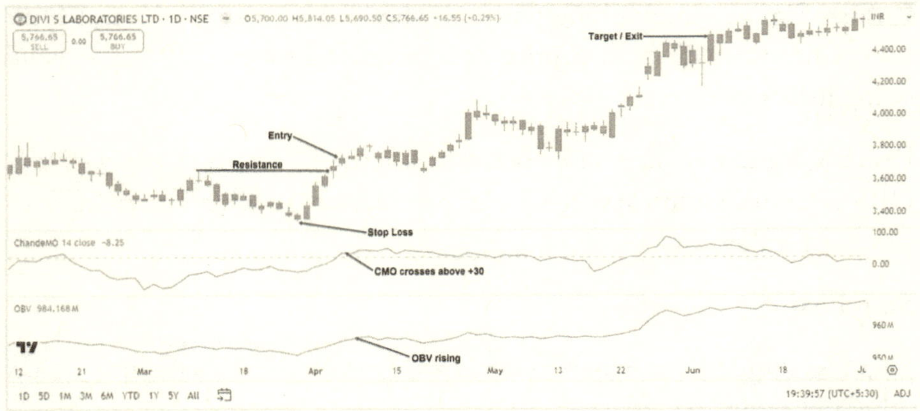

Miscellaneous Angles

For traders seeking to expand their analytical toolkit, this chapter provides an array of unconventional yet powerful trading strategies. "Alternative Angles" explores a diverse set of indicators and methods designed to uncover hidden opportunities in the market.

The chapter begins with Fibonacci Retracements, a time-tested tool for identifying key support and resistance levels based on natural ratios. It then delves into the Average True Range (ATR) for gauging market volatility, helping traders set stop-losses and profit targets more effectively. Tools like the Volume Oscillator and Donchian Channels are introduced as innovative ways to measure volume dynamics and breakout potential, respectively.

Beginners will also encounter strategies built around less common indicators, such as Williams %R, Relative Vigor Index (RVI), and the Money Flow Index (MFI). Each method is explained with practical examples, showing how these tools can be integrated into a cohesive trading plan. By embracing these alternative angles, traders will gain a broader perspective on market behavior, equipping them to navigate complex market conditions with greater agility and insight.

75

Fibonacci Retracement Strategy

The Fibonacci series is well known today; you can Google for more details. Some Fibonacci ratios are fundamental and widely used in trading: 61.8%, 38.2%, and 23.6%. We will use these as Support/ Resistance.

Entry:

Bullish Signal: Enter long positions when the price retraces to a Fibonacci support level and shows signs of reversal, indicating potential buying opportunities.

Bearish Signal: Enter short positions when the price retraces to a Fibonacci resistance level and exhibits signs of reversal, suggesting potential selling opportunities.

Stop Loss:

Stop loss should be based on the next fibo level or any other indicator.

Exit Rules:

Profit Target: The profit target should be based on your risk - reward ratio. It could be a specific percentage gain or the next fibo level.

Trailing Stop: You can trail stop - loss to maximize your profit and ride the full momentum as the price moves in your favor.

Risk Management:

Position Sizing: Determine the appropriate size based on your risk tolerance and account size. You should park only 5% of your Capital at a time.

Risk - Reward Ratio: Ensure that your potential profit is significantly greater than your potential loss for each trade. It would help if you kept your Risk - Reward ratio at least 1:2.

Example:

For a Bullish example, refer to the attached chart of DRREDDY. We have plotted Fibo levels by joining the Low (Close of 03rd November 2023) and High (Close of 27th February 2024). On 04thJune 2024, the stock touched a fibo level of 0.382 and started to bounce back the next day (Green candle). We take entry (buy stock) on 07th June 2024 at 1212.00 (when Price crosses above fibo level 0.618) with a stop loss at 1140.00 (Previous fibo level, i.e. 0.382) and Target of 1356.00 (R: R 1:2). The Risk: Reward achieved is 1:2 and the Target hit on 15th July, 24 with 11.88% profit on deployed capital.

76

ATR (Average True Range) Breakout Strategy

The ATR indicator measures market/stock volatility and identifies potential breakout levels. A stock with a high level of volatility has a higher ATR, and a stock with a lower level of volatility has a lower ATR. You can use the ATR value to set stop - loss orders and profit targets.

Entry:

Bullish Signal: Enter a long position when the Price breaks out above a recent high or previous resistance with high volatility (increasing ATR), indicating a bullish breakout and potential trend continuation.

Bearish Signal: Enter a short position when the Price breaks below a recent low or previous support with high volatility (increasing ATR), signaling a bearish breakout and potential trend continuation.

Stop Loss:

Stop loss should be 2 x ATR, i.e., 2 times the value of ATR.

Exit Rules:

Profit Target: Your profit target should be based on your risk - reward ratio. It could be a specific percentage gain or the next Support/Resistance.

Trailing Stop: You can trail a stop loss by using ATR to maximize your profit and ride the full momentum as the price moves in your favor.

Risk Management:

Position Sizing: Determine the appropriate size based on your risk tolerance and account size. You should park only 5% of your Capital at a time.

Risk - Reward Ratio: Ensure that your potential profit is significantly greater than your potential loss for each trade. It would help if you kept your Risk - Reward ratio at least 1:2.

Example:

For a Bullish example, refer to the attached chart of Apollo Hospitals. On 01ˢᵗ June 2023, the ATR increased the last few days and showed rising volatility in the stock - price also broke out of the previous swing high (previous resistance). Price action and ATR confirms the strong bullish trend. We take entry (buy stock) at 4815.00 with a stop loss at 4575.00 (2 x ATR) and a Target of 5300.00 (R: R 1:2). The Risk: Reward achieved is 1:2 and the Target hit on 06ᵗʰ July 2023 with 10.07% profit on deployed capital.

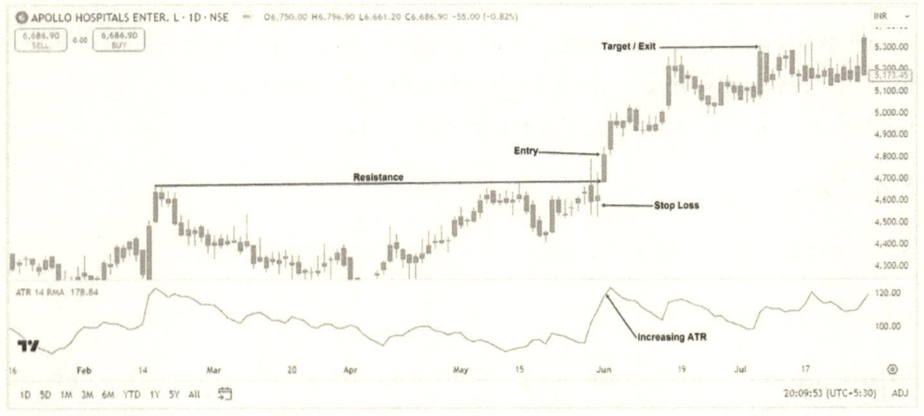

77

Williams %R (Williams Percent Range) Strategy

The Williams %R indicator helps identify overbought and oversold market conditions. You can combine Williams %R signals with other technical indicators or price patterns to confirm and filter out false signals.

Entry:

Bullish Signal: Enter a long position when the Williams %R crosses above the oversold threshold (e.g., - 80), indicating a potential bullish reversal.

Bearish Signal: Enter a short position when the Williams %R crosses below the overbought threshold (e.g., - 20), signaling a potential bearish reversal.

Stop Loss:

Stop loss should be previous Swing low/high, Support/Resistance, or any other indicator.

Exit Rules:

Profit Target: Your profit target should be based on your risk - reward ratio. It could be a specific percentage gain or the next Support/Resistance.

Trailing Stop: You can trail stop - loss to maximize your profit and ride the full momentum as the price moves in your favor.

Risk Management:

Position Sizing: Determine the appropriate size based on your risk tolerance and account size. You should park only 5% of your Capital at a time.

Risk - Reward Ratio: Ensure that your potential profit is significantly greater than your potential loss for each trade. It would help if you kept your Risk - Reward ratio at least 1:2.

Example:

For a Bullish example, refer to the attached chart of Apollo Tyres. On 20th August 2024, the Williams %R line crosses above - 80, which indicates a possible reversal from the oversold zone. We take entry (buy stock) at 499.00 with a stop loss at 475.00 (Previous swing low) and the Target of 550.00 (R: R 1:2). The Risk: reward achieved is 1:2, and the Target hit on 26[th]September 2024 with a 10.00% profit on deployed capital.

78

Volume Oscillator Strategy

The volume oscillator helps to identify changes in volume momentum. It is an indicator made up of two - volume moving averages, one fast (14 - period) and the other slow (28 - period).

Entry:

Bullish Signal: Enter a long position when the volume oscillator crosses above zero, indicating increasing buying volume and potential bullish momentum. Confirm trade with other indicators or Price Breakout.

Bearish Signal: Enter a short position when the volume oscillator crosses below zero, signaling increasing selling volume and potential bearish momentum. Confirm trade with other indicators or Price Breakdown.

Stop Loss:

Stop loss should be previous Swing low/high, Support/Resistance, or any other indicator.

Exit Rules:

Profit Target: Your profit target should be based on your risk - reward ratio. It could be a specific percentage gain or the next Support/Resistance.

Trailing Stop: You can trail stop - loss to maximize your profit and ride the full momentum as the price moves in your favor.

Risk Management:

Position Sizing: Determine the appropriate size based on your risk tolerance and account size. You should park only 5% of your Capital at a time.

Risk - Reward Ratio: Ensure that your potential profit is significantly greater than your potential loss for each trade. It would help if you kept your Risk - Reward ratio at least 1:2.

Example:

For a Bullish example, refer to the attached chart of Astral Ltd. On 05th May2023, the Volume Oscillator crosses above 0, and the Price breaks out of the previous swing high. We take entry (buy stock) at 1510.00 with a stop loss at 1380.00 (Previous swing low) and a Target of 1770.00 (R: R 1:2). The Risk: reward achieved is 1:2, and the Target hit on 26th May2023 with a 17.22% profit on deployed capital.

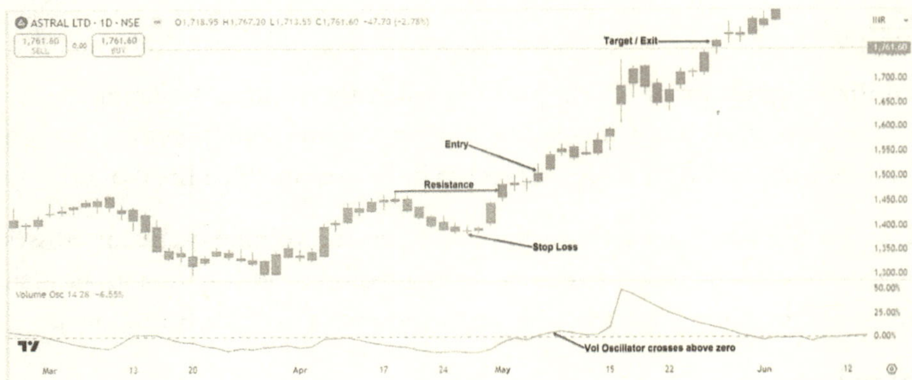

79

Volume Weighted
Moving Average (VWMA) Strategy

The Volume - Weighted Moving Average (VWMA) weighs each Price based on its trading volume and is, therefore, very important.

Entry:

Bullish Signal: Enter a long position when the Price crosses above the VWMA, indicating increasing buying pressure and potential trend continuation.

Bearish Signal: Enter a short position when the price crosses below the VWMA, signaling increasing selling pressure and potential trend continuation.

Stop Loss:

Stop loss should be previous Swing low/high, Support/Resistance, or any other indicator.

Exit Rules:

Profit Target: Your profit target should be based on your risk - reward ratio. It could be a specific percentage gain or the next Support/Resistance.

Trailing Stop: You can trail stop - loss to maximize your profit and ride the full momentum as the price moves in your favor.

Risk Management:

Position Sizing: Determine the appropriate size based on your risk tolerance and account size. You should park only 5% of your Capital at a time.

Risk - Reward Ratio: Ensure that your potential profit is significantly greater than your potential loss for each trade. It would help if you kept your Risk - Reward ratio at least 1:2.

Example:

For a Bullish example, refer to the attached chart of AUROPHARMA. On 26th March 2024, the candle closes above 20 VWMA. We take entry (buy stock) at 1055.00 with a stop loss at 980.00 (Previous swing low) and a Target of 1205.00 (R: R 1:2). The Risk: reward achieved is 1:2, and the Target hit on 18th May 2024 with 14.22% profit on deployed capital.

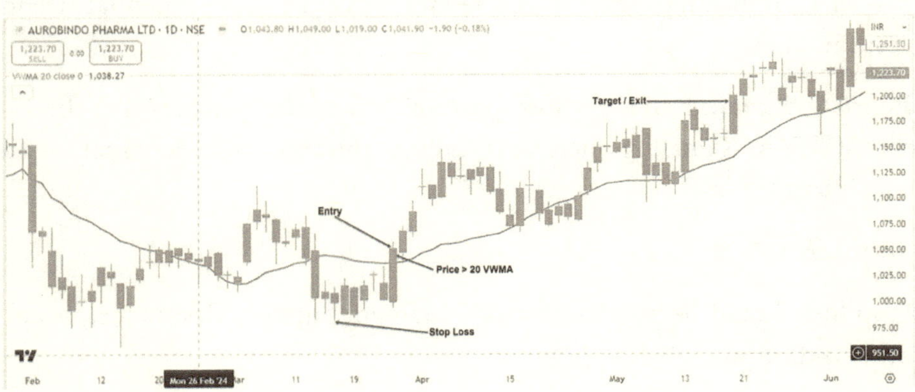

80

Donchian Channel Breakout Strategy

Donchian Channels plot the highest high and lowest low over a specified period (e.g., 20 periods). Use Donchian Channel width to gauge volatility and anticipate potential breakout or breakdown points. You can take a trade if the Price breaks out of the Higher/Lower Band of the Donchian Channel.

Entry:

Bullish Signal: Enter a long position when the Price breaks out above the mid - line Donchian Channel, indicating a bullish breakout and potential trend continuation.

Bearish Signal: Enter a short position when the Price breaks below the mid - line Donchian Channel, signaling a bearish breakout and potential trend continuation.

Stop Loss:

Stop loss should be the previous Swing low/high or upper/lower line of the Donchian Channel.

Exit Rules:

Profit Target: Your profit target should be based on your risk - reward ratio. It could be a specific percentage gain or the next Support/Resistance.

Trailing Stop: You can trail stop - loss to maximize your profit and ride the full momentum as the price moves in your favor.

Risk Management:

Position Sizing: Determine the appropriate size based on your risk tolerance and account size. You should park only 5% of your Capital at a time.

Risk - Reward Ratio: Ensure that your potential profit is significantly greater than your potential loss for each trade. It would help if you kept your Risk - Reward ratio at least 1:2.

Example:

For a Bullish example, refer to the attached HBL Power System Ltd chart. On 23rd May2023, the candle crosses above the midline of the Donchian Channel. We take entry (buy stock) at 110.00 with a stop loss at 99.00 (Lower line of Donchian Channel) and a Target of 132.00 (R: R 1:2). The Risk: reward achieved is 1:2, and the Target hit on 06th June 2023 with a 20.00% profit on deployed capital.

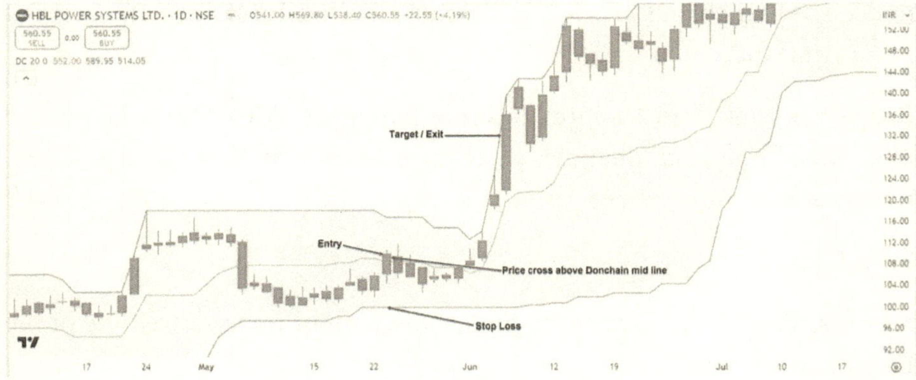

81

Relative Vigor Index (RVI) Strategy

The Relative Vigor Index (RVI) tool measures the strength of a trend based on the closing prices relative to the trading range. The RVI has two lines (Green and red). The Green line is the RVI line, and the Red line (4 VWMA of RVI) is the Signal line.

Entry:

Bullish Signal: Enter a long position when the RVI crosses above zero. The RVI line should also be above the signal line, indicating bullish momentum.

Bearish Signal: Enter a short position when the RVI crosses below zero. The signal line should be above the RVI line, signaling bearish momentum.

Stop Loss:

Stop loss should be previous Swing low/high, Support/Resistance, or any other indicator.

Exit Rules:

Profit Target: You can set a profit target for your risk - reward ratio. It could be a specific percentage gain or the next Support/Resistance.

Trailing Stop: You can trail stop - loss to maximize your profit and ride the full momentum as the price moves in your favor.

Risk Management:

Position Sizing: Determine the appropriate size based on your risk tolerance and account size. You should park only 5% of your Capital at a time.

Risk - Reward Ratio: Ensure that your potential profit is significantly greater than your potential loss for each trade. It would help if you kept your Risk - Reward ratio at least 1:2.

Example:

For a bullish example, refer to the attached chart for Balkrishna Industries. The RVI has been moving upwards for a few days, crossing above 0 (zero) on 18th March 2024, but we are waiting for bullish price action. On 05th April 2024, the RVI is positive, the RVI line (Green line) is trading above the signal line (Red line), and the candle breaks out the previous swing high. We take entry (buy stock) at 2405.00 with a stop loss at 2190.00 (Previous Swing Low) and a Target of 2840.00 (R: R 1:2). The Risk: Reward achieved is 1:2, and the Target hit on 21st May 2024 with 18.09% profit on deployed capital.

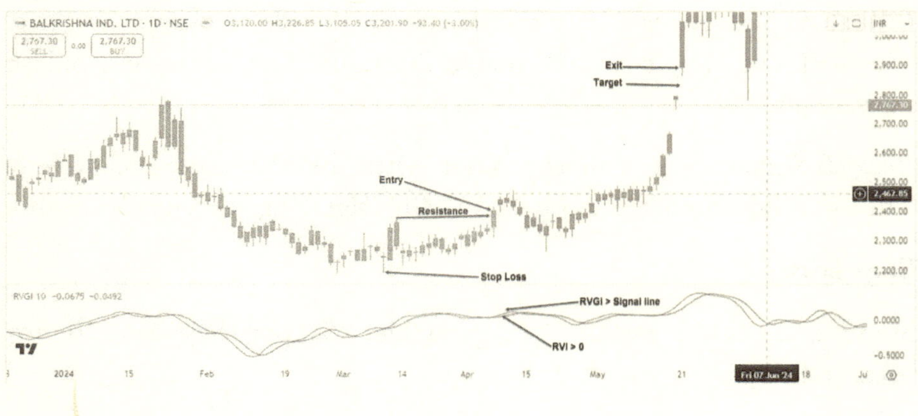

82

Detrended Price Oscillator (DPO) Strategy

The Detrended Price Oscillator (DPO) is used to identify cycles and potential trend reversals. It shows the difference between a past price and a simple moving average. In contrast to other price oscillators, DPO is not a momentum indicator. It is designed to identify cycles with their peaks and troughs.

Entry:

Bullish Signal: Enter a long position when the DPO crosses above zero, indicating bullish momentum.

Bearish Signal: Enter a short position when the DPO crosses below zero, signaling bearish momentum.

Stop Loss:

Stop loss should be previous swing low/high, Support/Resistance, or any other indicator.

Exit Rules:

Profit Target: Your profit target should be based on your risk - reward ratio. It could be a specific percentage gain or the next Support/Resistance.

Trailing Stop: You can trail stop - loss to maximize your profit and ride the full momentum as the price moves in your favor.

Risk Management:

Position Sizing: Determine the appropriate size based on your risk tolerance and account size. You should park only 5% of your Capital at a time.

Risk - Reward Ratio: Ensure that your potential profit is significantly greater than your potential loss for each trade. It would help if you kept your Risk - Reward ratio at least 1:2.

Example:

For a Bullish example, refer to the attached chart of the Bank of India. On 13th November 2023, the DPO crosses above 0 (zero), and the candle is Green (bullish). We take entry (buy stock) at 108.00 with a stop loss at 86.00 (Previous Swing Low) and a Target of 152.00 (R: R 1:2). The Risk: reward achieved is 1:2, and the Target hit on 02nd February 2024 with 40.74% profit on deployed capital.

83

Choppiness Index Strategy

The Choppiness Index (CI) is a technical analysis tool used to identify whether the market is trending or ranging. The CI values range between 0 and 100, with a low value signaling a strong trend (directional trending) and a high value indicating consolidation/ranging. A CI above 50 indicates a consolidation/range - bound market; therefore, one should avoid trading.

Entry:

Bullish Signal: Enter trend - following trades when the Choppiness Index is below a certain threshold (e.g., 50) and there is Price action (Price breakout previous swing high or Resistance), indicating a trending market.

Bearish Signal: Enter trend - following trades when the Choppiness Index is below a certain threshold (e.g., 50) and there is Price action (Price breakdown previous swing Low or Support), indicating a trending market.

Stop Loss:

Stop loss should be previous swing low/high, Support/Resistance, or any other indicator.

Exit Rules:

Profit Target: Your profit target should be based on your risk - reward ratio. It could be a specific percentage gain or the next Support/Resistance.

Trailing Stop: You can trail stop - loss to maximize your profit and ride the full momentum as the price moves in your favor.

Risk Management:

Position Sizing: Determine the appropriate size based on your risk tolerance and account size. You should park only 5% of your Capital at a time.

Risk - Reward Ratio: Ensure that your potential profit is significantly greater than your potential loss for each trade. It would help if you kept your Risk - Reward ratio at least 1:2.

Example:

For a Bullish example, refer to the attached chart of Bata India Ltd. On 21st April 23, the CI line crosses below 50, the Price breaks out of the previous swing high, and the candle is Green (bullish). We take entry (buy stock) at 1480.00 with a stop loss at 1380.00 (Previous Swing Low) and a Target of 1685.00 (R: R 1:2). The Risk: reward achieved is 1:2, and the Target hit on 07th July 23 with 13.85% profit on deployed capital.

84

Ultimate Oscillator Divergence Strategy

The Ultimate Oscillator is a momentum oscillator designed to capture momentum across three different time frames (7, 14, 28). It combines short‑term, medium‑term, and long‑term oscillators to identify potential trend reversals.

Entry:

Bullish Signal: Enter a long position when there is bullish divergence, i.e., UO is making higher lows, and Price is making Lower lows. The Ultimate Oscillator crosses above a certain threshold (e.g., 50), indicating bullish momentum, and there is price action (Price/Pattern breakout).

Bearish Signal: Enter a short position when there is a bearish divergence, i.e., UO is making Lower highs, Price is making higher highs, the Ultimate Oscillator crosses below a certain threshold (e.g., 50), signaling bearish momentum, and there is price action (Price/Pattern Breakdown).

Stop Loss:

Stop loss should be previous swing low/high, Support/Resistance, or any other indicator.

Exit Rules:

Profit Target: Your profit target should be based on your risk‑reward ratio. It could be a specific percentage gain or the next Support/Resistance.

Trailing Stop: You can trail stop‑loss to maximize your profit and ride the full momentum as the price moves in your favor.

Risk Management:

Position Sizing: Determine the appropriate size based on your risk tolerance and account size. You should park only 5% of your Capital at a time.

Risk - Reward Ratio: Ensure that your potential profit is significantly greater than your potential loss for each trade. It would help if you kept your Risk - Reward ratio at least 1:2.

Example:

For a Bullish example, refer to the attached chart of Bharat Dynamics. Between the last week of Sep 2023 and the last week of Oct 2023, Ultimate Oscillator is making higher lows & Price is making Lower lows, i.e., there is a bullish divergence; on 13th November 2023, the UO is trading above 50. The Price breaks out of the previous swing high. We take entry (buy stock) at 541.00 with a stop loss at 450.00 (Previous Swing Low) and a Target of 724.00 (R: R 1:2). The Risk: Reward achieved is 1:2, and the Target hit on 18thDec2023 with 33.83% profit on deployed capital.

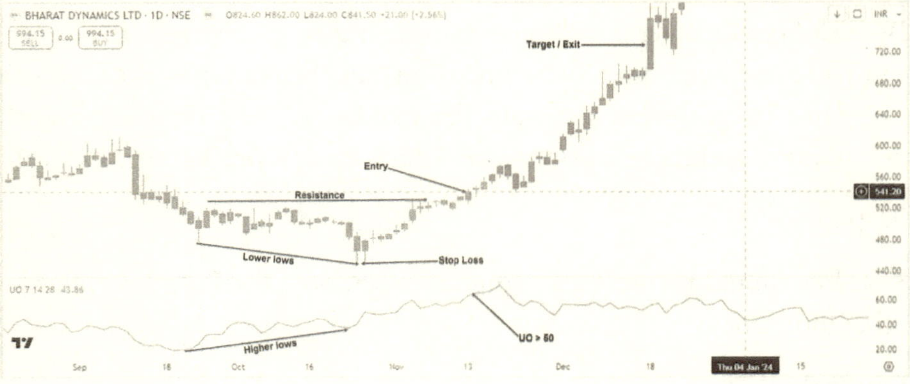

85

Rate of Change (ROC) Strategy

The Rate of Change (ROC) is a momentum technical indicator that measures the percentage change in price over a specified period.

Entry:

Bullish Signal: Enter a long position when the ROC crosses above zero, indicating bullish momentum.

Bearish Signal: Enter a short position when the ROC crosses below zero, signaling bearish momentum.

Stop Loss:

Stop loss should be previous swing low/high, Support/Resistance, or any other indicator.

Exit Rules:

Profit Target: Your profit target should be based on your risk - reward ratio. It could be a specific percentage gain or the next Support/Resistance.

Trailing Stop: You can trail stop - loss to maximize your profit and ride the full momentum as the price moves in your favor.

Risk Management:

Position Sizing: Determine the appropriate size based on your risk tolerance and account size. You should park only 5% of your Capital at a time.

Risk - Reward Ratio: Ensure that your potential profit is significantly greater than your potential loss for each trade. It would help if you kept your Risk - Reward ratio at least 1:2.

Example:

For a bullish example, refer to the attached chart for Britannia Industries. On 6th Nov - 2023, the ROC lines crossed above 0 (zero), and on 07th Nov - 2023, the Price broke out of the previous swing high. We took an entry (buy stock) at 4660.00 with a stop loss at 4340.00 (Previous Swing Low) and a Target of 5300.00 (R: R 1:2). The Risk: reward achieved is 1:2, and the Target hit on 28th Dec - 2023 with a 13.73% profit on deployed capital.

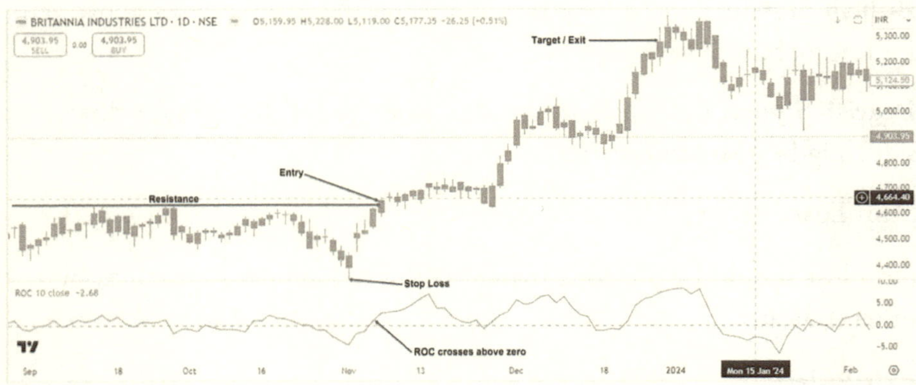

86

Money Flow Index (MFI) Strategy

The Money Flow Index (MFI) measures the strength of buying and selling pressure. It is a momentum and volume indicator.

Entry:

Bullish Signal: Enter a long position when the MFI exceeds 50, indicating potential buying pressure and strong bullish momentum.

Bearish Signal: Enter a short position when the MFI exceeds 50, signaling potential selling pressure and strong bearish momentum.

Stop Loss:

Stop loss should be previous swing low/high, Support/Resistance, or any other indicator.

Exit Rules:

Profit Target: Your profit target should be based on your risk - reward ratio. It could be a specific percentage gain or the next Support/Resistance.

Trailing Stop: You can trail stop - loss to maximize your profit and ride the full momentum as the price moves in your favor.

Risk Management:

Position Sizing: Determine the appropriate size based on your risk tolerance and account size. You should park only 5% of your Capital at a time.

Risk - Reward Ratio: Ensure that your potential profit is significantly greater than your potential loss for each trade. It would help if you kept your Risk - Reward ratio at least 1:2.

Example:

For a Bullish example, refer to the attached chart of Coforge Ltd. On 23rd March 2024, the MFI line crossed above 50, indicating potential buying pressure and strong bullish momentum. We take entry (buy stock) at 5067.00 with a stop loss at 4285.00 (Previous Swing Low) and a Target of 6630.00 (R: R 1:2). The Risk: reward achieved is 1:2, and the Target hit on 06th Sep - 2024 with 30.85% profit on deployed capital.

87

Standard Deviation Channel Strategy

The Standard Deviation Channels plot bands based on price volatility to identify potential support and resistance levels. The slope of the line designates an upward or downward trend.

Entry:

Bullish Signal: Enter a long position when the price touches or falls below the lower Standard Deviation Channel. This indicates potential oversold conditions and a bounce back to the mean or upper band.

Bearish Signal: Enter a short position when the price touches or rises above the upper Standard Deviation Channel, signaling potential overbought conditions and a retracement back to the mean or lower band.

Stop Loss:

Stop loss should be previous swing low/high, Support/Resistance, or any other indicator.

Exit Rules:

Profit Target: Your profit target should be based on your risk - reward ratio. It could be a specific percentage gain or the next Support/Resistance.

Trailing Stop: You can trail stop - loss to maximize your profit and ride the full momentum as the price moves in your favor.

Risk Management:

Position Sizing: Determine the appropriate size based on your risk tolerance and account size. You should park only 5% of your Capital at a time.

Risk - Reward Ratio: Ensure that your potential profit is significantly greater than your potential loss for each trade. It would help if you kept your Risk - Reward ratio at least 1:2.

Example:

Refer to the attached Container Corp (CONCOR) chart for a Bullish example. On 20th Mar - 24, the Price crossed below the lower band of SDC (Standard Deviation Channel) and bounced back. We take entry (buy stock) on 21st March 2024, at 875.00 with a stop loss at 815.00 (Previous Swing Low) and a Target of 995.00 (R: R 1:2). The Risk: Reward achieved is 1:2 and Target hit on 25th Apr - 24 with 13.71% profit on deployed capital.

88

Fisher Transform Strategy

The Fisher Transform indicator converts price data into a Gaussian normal distribution to identify potential trend reversals.

Entry:

Bullish Signal: Enter a long position when the Fisher Transform crosses above the oversold threshold (e.g.,- 1), indicating potential bullish momentum.

Bearish Signal: Enter a short position when the Fisher Transform crosses below the overbought threshold (e.g., 1), signaling potential bearish momentum.

Stop Loss:

Stop loss should be previous swing low/high, Support/Resistance, or any other indicator.

Exit Rules:

Profit Target: Your profit target should be based on your risk - reward ratio. It could be a specific percentage gain or the next Support/Resistance.

Trailing Stop: You can trail stop - loss to maximize your profit and ride the full momentum as the price moves in your favor.

Risk Management:

Position Sizing: Determine the appropriate size based on your risk tolerance and account size. You should park only 5% of your Capital at a time.

Risk - Reward Ratio: Ensure that your potential profit is significantly greater than your potential loss for each trade. It would help if you kept your Risk - Reward ratio at least 1:2.

Example:

For a Bullish example, refer to the attached chart of Coromandel International. On 04th Apr - 24, the Fisher Transform crosses above - 1, indicating a bullish reversal; we await Price action. On 05th Apr - 24, the Price breaks out of the previous swing high. We take entry (buy stock) at 1162.00 with a stop loss at 1036.00 (Previous Swing Low) and a Target of 1414.00 (R: R 1:2). The Risk: Reward achieved is 1:2, and Target hit on 10th June - 24 with 21.69% profit on deployed capital.

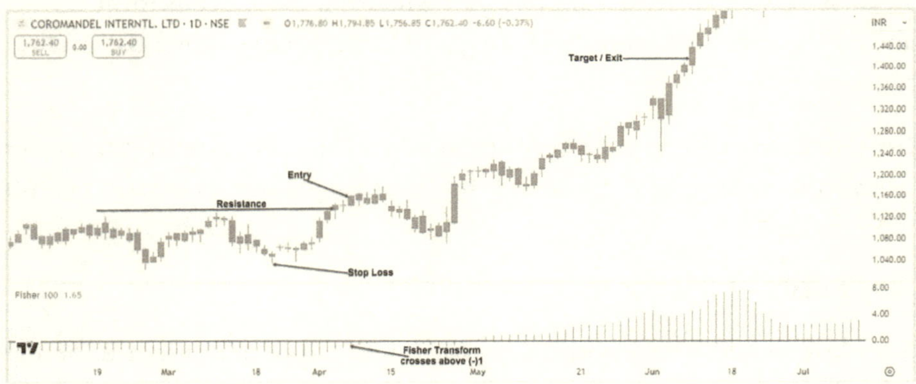

89

Volume – Weighted Average Price (VWAP) Strategy

The Volume - Weighted Average Price (VWAP) indicator is used to identify potential support and resistance levels based on average price and volume

Entry:

Bullish Signal: Enter a long position when the earlier trend is bearish or sideways, and the price crosses/closes above the VWAP, indicating potential bullish momentum. For additional confirmation, look for a previous swing high breakout.

Bearish Signal: Enter a short position when the earlier trend is bullish or sideways, and the price crosses/closes below the VWAP, signaling potential bearish momentum. For additional confirmation, look for a previous swing low breakdown.

Stop Loss:

Stop loss should be previous swing low/high, Support/Resistance, or any other indicator.

Exit Rules:

Profit Target: Your profit target should be based on your risk - reward ratio. It could be a specific percentage gain or the next Support/Resistance.

Trailing Stop: You can trail stop - loss to maximize your profit and ride the full momentum as the price moves in your favor.

Risk Management:

Position Sizing: Determine the appropriate size based on your risk tolerance and account size. You should park only 5% of your Capital at a time.

Risk - Reward Ratio: Ensure that your potential profit is significantly greater than your potential loss for each trade. It would help if you kept your Risk - Reward ratio at least 1:2.

Example:

For a bullish example, refer to the attached chart for Tata Motors. The trend has been sideways for the last two to three months. On 03rd Oct - 23, the Price crossed above VWAP and broke out of the previous swing high. We took entry (buy stock) at 667.00 with a stop loss at 608.00 (Previous Swing Low) and a Target of 785.00 (R: R 1:2). The Risk: reward achieved is 1:2, and the Target hit on 29th Dec - 23 with 17.69% profit on deployed capital.

Disclaimer

Trading in the stock market is subject to market risk, read all the documents carefully. Please analyze your risk profile before taking any trade. This book is only for educational purposes. This is not an advisory book and there is no Buy or Sell advice. The content of this book is only for educational purposes. Author's comments are an expression of opinion only. It is highly recommended to consult your investment advisor before making any investment decision, and that you should confirm the facts on your own before making any important investment commitment.

Special Thank You

This book is the best part and core of my heart to feel the emotions that made me strong throughout the life. I cannot express in words what you two mean for me but found a page suitable for you both to dedicate my love.

A Husband and a Father is proud to hold you in life forever. A success is owned only by getting their support which paved the way to accomplish new vision. My heart is my wife **Neha** who has been my hardest rock, initiator and supporter throughout my life in all decisions. She is the role model that made my life into a happy home. My lovely daughter **Riddhi** is my soul that overcomes my hard work with joy and laughter. Her existence is my determination to be responsible in the future and keep growing. My aim is to give them a better prospect in life.

This book is an emotional, professional and personal bond in my career that molds in a beautiful way to embark my knowledge. This book is a tribute to both of you, a reflection of the strength, love, and hope you bring into my life. Thank you for being my everything. This journey is as much yours as it is mine.

An author is the person who creates a vision to write a book, and here let us introduce our inspiring, motivational, and knowledgeable person, **Atulesh Sinha,** who has put in an effort to ease traders through this book. He is a renowned coach, trader, and expert in the infrastructure field with 17+ years of professional experience. He believes in the thought that "you should not work for money"; "money should work for you." This thought process inspired him to join the stock market. He has taken the expertise and tried trading styles, including swing trading, mid-term investing, and long-term investing, which allows him to develop a comprehensive understanding of how various strategies work in different timeframes.

A person who has started their journey from civil engineering at Prayagraj, Uttar Pradesh. He has built life in a disciplined way from his dad, who served the nation as an Indian Army and became a supporter of all the individuals as kindness by following Mother's nature. We can also see his efforts in a knowledgeable way through his expertise in trade from the past 9+ years, which is reflected in this book.

Beyond trading, Atulesh is deeply passionate about empowering others and sharing knowledge (Vidhya woh dhan hai jo kharch karne se aur badhti hai). His goal is to provide practical, actionable strategies that traders of all experience levels can use to enhance their performance in the markets. He views the process of learning and mastering the markets as an ongoing journey, and this philosophy is what he hopes to instill in every reader of this book. He firmly believes that trading is not just about making profits but also about developing the right mindset, discipline, and continuous self-improvement.

Atulesh is a husband of a loving life partner, Neha, a father blessed with a daughter, Riddhi, Nature loving and Spiritual person. He wanted to be an example and guide for the newcomers in the trade and become successful by using these strategies, which are tested thoroughly by different traders.

He continues to explore the world of trading, always searching for new methods, tools, and perspectives to enhance his knowledge and the success of his students. His aim is to remake the "trader" with the same vision and make himself a beneficiary with his own ideas and wisdom.

For more information, please connect with him at **www.atuleshsinha. com**.